INTERNATIONAL AFFAIRS: AN ASIAN PERSPECTIVE

(SHORT ESSAYS)

Haroon Pasha

INTERNATIONAL AFFAIRS
AN
ASIAN PERSPECTIVE

(SHORT ESSAYS)

FOR MOTHER

AND

MOTHER OF MY CHILDREN

(THEIR LOVE IS AN ETERNAL SOURCE OF INSPIRATION FOR ME)

Preface

This book is hard earning of my efforts where I continuously researched International issues influencing the region and policies of different states of Asian Continent. Why Asia is important? Why this century is called as an Asian century? The phenomenal rise of China and reawakening of the Russia has created much scepticism in the west. The ASEAN countries and India are constantly expanding their sphere of influence in the region. Turkey and Pakistan are gaining importance due to their centrality in the Turkish speaking countries and CPEC project respectively. Arab Spring and constant transitional political situation in Iran and Afghanistan has made this region as the most volatile region of the World. The aftershocks of Arab Spring have jolted the absolute monarchies of the Gulf region. This book will help the students, professionals and scholars to have a better understanding about the Asian politics with International context.

HAROON PASHA

APRIL 2021

Part I

China

Part II

South Asia

Part III

Russia

Part IV

International Affairs

Part V

Middle East

Part VI

Asia Pacific

China

Deng Xiaoping and Chinese Modernization

Background

Deng Xiao Ping is considered as the father of modern China. He was the visionary who set the pace of Chinese growth and all the present pay modernization present in the Chinese economy was due to his foresight. China is the country of miracles and the first miracle was its establishment in 1949. Later on, Chairman Mao decided to switch from an agricultural economy to an industrial economy. For this purpose "Great Leap Forward" project was kick-started. Later on, for the complete purge of imperialism, the "Cultural Revolution" was perpetrated. All these success and failure revolutions have very deep impacts on the Chinese people.

Chu Enlai and Four Modernization Programme

Four Modernizations, four areas of development which are agriculture, industry, science and technology, and defence that China focused on beginning in the late 1970s intending to fully modernize those sectors by the end of the 20th century. The embrace of the Four Modernizations and the related emphasis on economic development marked a significant departure from the country's policies immediately before this, which had been primarily focused on ideology. Prime Minister Chu Enlai was the first person who felt the need for this in 1964 but he was unable to materialize his dreams later on in 1975 this dream was materialized in the fourth National Congress when Chinese leadership decided to have a focus on a development model for their economy.

What are four Modernizations?

Although China was a Communist country and its economy was centrally managed. The Four Modernizations were not prioritized by the government, however, until after Mao died in September 1976 and the cadre of party officials known as the Gang of Four, which had opposed the Four Modernizations, was purged shortly thereafter. Championed by Deng, the Four Modernizations were enshrined in the Communist Party constitution at the Eleventh Party Congress in 1977 and the state's constitution at the Fifth National People's Congress in 1978 and became the basis for the policies that contributed to the country's impressive growth in the years to come. These four modernizations are

1. Agriculture

2. Industry

3. Defence

4. Science & Technology

Chinese leadership decided that these above mentioned four fields are the main growth stimulus for the country. This modernization had taken almost three decades to give dividends.

Four-Modernization Program and Its Impacts on Foreign Policy of China

Although, President Trump has blamed China as a "revisionist power" and a complete "rival" in the trade and International system China, on the other hand, had an agrarian economy and they transform their economy during the "Great Leap Forward". Western thinkers and political scholars are very critical of the policies of the Chinese present regime, especially under President Xi Xing ping. The Belt and Road (BRI) initiative is the biggest project of trade in human history. Initially, it will link 65 countries with China through Land and Sea routes. According to one estimate, it will generate a US $ 21 Trillion economy as an outcome of it. Half of humanity will be linked through it. China's Belt and Road Initiative (BRI), sometimes referred to as the New Silk Road, is one of the most ambitious infrastructure projects ever conceived. Launched in 2013 by President Xi Jinping, the vast collection of development and investment initiatives would stretch from East Asia to Europe, significantly expanding China's economic and political influence.

Some analysts see the project as an unsettling extension of China's rising power, and as the costs of many of the projects have skyrocketed, the opposition has grown in some countries. Meanwhile, the United States shares the concern of some in Asia that the BRI could be a proxy for a China-led regional development and military expansion. Under President Donald J. Trump, Washington has raised alarm over Beijing's actions, but it has struggled to offer governments in the region a more appealing economic vision. So this post BRI world will have very deep-rooted impacts on the West and its policies. The Chinese model has been proven successful in the Post Corona world. China has maintained its growth rate at around 6 % per annum. According to the USA think tanks and economic intelligence units report China will become the No 1 economy of the world in 2039 but after dealing with Corona swiftly now China will supersede the USA in this decade.

China is following the golden principle of non-interference in the internal issues of other countries and resolving all international disputes through negotiations. Trade is the weapon in the arsenal of China where they are to resolve all the issues; it is the rule of the Chinese foreign policy.

Rise of China and its global implications

Introduction

After the devastation of the world wars and major destructions inflected by the man-made lethal weapons, Europe decided to take a new leap forward in the direction of the development of the human race therefore, in 1951 European Coal and Steel Community was established, it was a time when bloodthirsty enemies joined their hands for cooperation. It was the first step in the direction of regional cooperation at the international level in the recent past. Large-scale deaths in WWI and WWII were eye-opening for the west. Euro integration was a step in the right direction at the right time when Europe has joined their hands for large-scale cooperation. This regional integration has a lot more gains than losses. ASEAN and E.U, besides China, has made miracles and uplifted the standard of their population and millions are pulled out 850 Million from poverty.

Asian Century

This 21st century is called the Asian century after the awakening of the sleeping dragon China. According to Ex CIA Deputy Director John Maclaughlin "There is no way to prevent China from becoming the world's largest economy. This is not my conclusion. It belongs to one of America's most respected economists, former Clinton administration Treasury Secretary and Harvard President Lawrence Summers, and I have no reason to doubt it.

The Chinese economy is based on cheap exports to the World and now the Chinese economy is the second-largest economy in the world after the USA. To slow down the progress of ever-expanding Chinese exports USA has imposed many tariff and non-tariff barriers. China has openly emphasized its exports based economy. Now the Belt and Road initiative (BRI) will connect 4 billion people and 68 countries. The ever increasing influence has raised many eyebrows in the west. The west has become sceptical about the Chinese influence and the peaceful rise of China is unacceptable for the western hegemony.

Chinese Rise and Global threats

The peaceful rise of China is unprecedented for the world especially since the US is not ready to surrender in front of the Soft power of China. Chinese leader Xi Jinping's declaration at the close of the National People's Congress in March 2018 that his country would never seek hegemony or engage in expansion is likely to ring hollow in Western corridors of power. Zeng Xiaoping was that Chinese visionary who dreamt about the Rise of China and he transformed the Chinese Economy from a small economy to a competitive free market economy. West was that many sceptics about the rise of China that they nurtured the wrong theories i.e. "String of pearls" against China where they wrongly projected the secret and nefarious design of China to dominate the world and change the world order. The USA and Europe misperceived China as a threat, otherwise, the rise of China is exemplary and they have traditions from the previous five thousand years that they don't involve in any confrontation even they resolve their issues amicably without fighting. There is no global strategic threat linked with the peaceful rise of China.

Balance of Power

The balance of power phenomenon is very old and it had more relevance in the 18th century, but now in the 21st century and a Unipolar world, its scope is very limited. The balance will remain between the USA and China because; although China is the biggest rival of the USA it is the biggest trade partner of the USA also.

Counter Measures

Although China is playing very tactfully USA is trying to engage her in different internal and external issues. Human Rights, Uyghur issues, Tibet Moment, Taiwan issue, South China Sea, intellectual property rights are the core internal and External issues in which the USA is trying to engage China.

Conclusion

History has very rare examples of this type of Balance of Power. Now China is emerging as the economic power of the world and it is a very peaceful rise. China is intellectually confronting with the USA and maximizing her goals but after the emergence of Trump as president and its administration's draconian actions against the Chinese trade. The balance of trade has been badly disturbed and The US has said it will increase tariff rates on $200bn worth of Chinese imports from 10% to 25% if the two sides don't strike a deal so all is the world is waiting for the next moves of the world two heavyweights. Biden administration has also promoted propaganda of the human rights violations in Xinjiang province and Hong Kong.

China has emerged successful against the Covid-19 and it has strengthened its production sector. Growth prospects for China going into 2021 are similarly high. The International Monetary Fund (IMF) projects China's 2021 growth at a staggering 8.1%, well ahead of the United States at 5.1%, and second only to India with a projected

11.5% growth. In addition to incredible growth, China has also surpassed the United States in terms of attracting foreign direct investment (FDI). In the coming years, China will surpass the USA as the No 1 economy in the world.

The Impacts of Cultural Revolution on China

Chinese Cultural Revolution

The Great Proletarian Cultural Revolution was a decade-long period of political and social chaos caused by Mao Zedong's bid to use the Chinese masses to reassert his control over the Communist party. Its bewildering complexity and almost unfathomable brutality were such that to this day historians struggle to make sense of everything that occurred during the period. However, Mao's decision to launch the "revolution" in May 1966 is now widely interpreted as an attempt to destroy his enemies. The Cultural Revolution, formally the Great Proletarian Cultural Revolution, was a sociopolitical movement in China from 1966 until 1976.

Launched by Mao Zedong, then Chairman of the Communist Party of China, its stated goal was to preserve 'true' Communist ideology in the country by purging remnants of capitalist and traditional elements from Chinese society, and to re-impose Maoist thought as the dominant ideology within the Party. The Revolution marked Mao's return to a position of power after the Great Leap Forward. The movement paralyzed

China politically and negatively affected the country's economy and society to a significant degree.

By February of 1967, China had descended into chaos. The purges had reached the level of army generals who dared to speak out against the excesses of the Cultural Revolution, and Red Guards groups were turning against one another and fighting in the streets. Mao's wife, Jiang Qing, encouraged the Red Guards to raid arms from the People's Liberation Army (PLA), and even to replace the army entirely if necessary.

By December of 1968, even Mao realized that the Cultural Revolution was spinning out of control. China's economy, already weakened by the Great Leap Forward, was faltering badly. Industrial production fell by 12% in just two years. In reaction, Mao issued a call for the "Down to the Countryside Movement," in which young cadres from the city were sent to live on farms and learn from the peasants. Although he spun this idea as a tool for levelling society Mao sought to disperse the Red Guards across the country so that they could not cause so much trouble anymore.

For the entire decade of the Cultural Revolution, schools in China did not operate; this left an entire generation with no formal education. All of the educated and professional people had been targets for re-education. Those that hadn't been killed were dispersed across the countryside, toiling on farms or working in labour camps. All sorts of antiquities and artefacts were taken from museums and private homes; they were destroyed as symbols of "old thinking." Priceless historical and religious texts also were burned to ashes. The exact number of people killed during the Cultural Revolution is unknown, but it was at least in the hundreds of thousands, if not millions. Many of the victims of public humiliation committed suicide, as well. Members of ethnic and religious minorities suffered disproportionately, including Tibetan Buddhists, Hui people, and Mongolians. Terrible mistakes and brutal violence mar the history of Communist China. The Cultural Revolution is among the worst of these incidents, not only because of the horrific human suffering inflicted but also because so many remnants of that country's great and ancient culture were willfully destroyed.

Threat Perception by India by Rise of China in the Region

Introduction

India and China are the oldest civilizations of the world and they are unparalleled in strategic thinking, defence technology, the art of war and realpolitik. The old thinkers like Chankia Kotalia Confucius and Sun Tzu are the founding fathers of the realism and tactics of modern warfare. India is a middle-order power, but its ever-ambitious desire to get the status of regional power has ambitious outcomes. The rise of India has been fully supported by the United States. The peaceful rise of China is unprecedented in recent history. The prevailing fascism in Indian society and the present government of BJP has a grand design to dominate the region and the Indian Ocean. Now after many missed opportunities, India has very limited options in hand to resettle the pace of peace because the unreceptive Modi government in India is very uneasy with the regional changes and they think that India has to unilaterally deal with the regional issues. All the neighbours of India are resisting the bullying attitude of India. The world will see an emergence of peaceful and prosperous South Asia if and only if China and India cooperate.

Background

China and India (including South Asia) are the leading countries of Asia and they represent nearly half of the world population. China emerged as a leading player in the trading world by opening its communist economy for trade with the world after the reformist vision of Den Xiaoping in 1979. Now China is the second-biggest economy in the world and up till 2050, it will be the No one economy in the world. On the other hand, India is the leading economy of Asia and the ambitious role of India as a regional power is being supported by the USA and European countries. The antagonistic posture of the emerging power of India is countering the peaceful rise of China and its vision of peaceful trade and cooperation. The rise of Hindu nationalism is another phenomenon. The threat perception of India and its skirmishes with China and Pakistan have highlighted the fault lines in India policy and its hostile and aggressive posture is a threat not only for the regional peace but for the world.

Economy

China and India are the two emerging economies in the world. As of 2019, China and India are the 2nd and 5th largest country in the world, respectively on a nominal basis. Both countries together share 19.46% and 27.18% of total global wealth in nominal and PPP terms, respectively. Among Asian countries, China and India together contribute more than half of Asia's GDP. The first target of China is to establish trade relations and capture new markets for raw material and consumption of its products.

China has signed a new deal with Iran where China is likely to gain much and the sphere of Chinese influence will extend to the Persian Gulf. After signing the proposed US $ 400 Billion agreements, Iran has announced to develop its railway line, which was planned to be built by India. The gas projects having the same fate because, India was failed to fulfil its obligations. In 2016 Iran, India and Afghanistan signed a deal to stipulate to expand their trade. Chinese presence is evident in banking, telecommunications, ports, railways and dozens of other projects. In exchange, China would receive a regular and, according to an Iranian official and an oil trader, heavily discounted supply of Iranian oil over the next 25 years. India can become a loser in this deal if India will not be able to secure its investments in major projects including Chahbahar port.

Regional Influence

India and China are ever-increasing their sphere of influence in the region by expanding their bilateral and multilateral agreements with the regional countries, but India had badly been outnumbered by the Chinese investment. China has started the biggest project of history under the nomenclature of the Belt and Road Initiative (BRI) which will connect more than 68 countries of the world through sea and land routes. This project will generate a turnover of around US $ 21 Trillion over the years. CPEC is also one offshoot of this project.

On The other hand, India is heavily investing in its strategic assets. Indian Navy is following a strategy of sea-control, which is "the ability to use the sea in reasonable safety." The Indian naval doctrine defines sea control as a capability to use a defined sea area, for a defined period, for a defined purpose, and simultaneously deny the sea to the enemy. Sea control is exercised using a combination of capital-intensive ships, fixed-wing aircraft, helicopters and amphibious capabilities. It is an expensive affair and requires sustained modernization. On the other hand, China has developed Sea Lanes of Communication (SLOC) for imports of raw material and exports of its finished goods. In 2017 China has established its 1st international military post in Djibouti (Africa).

Djibouti Port

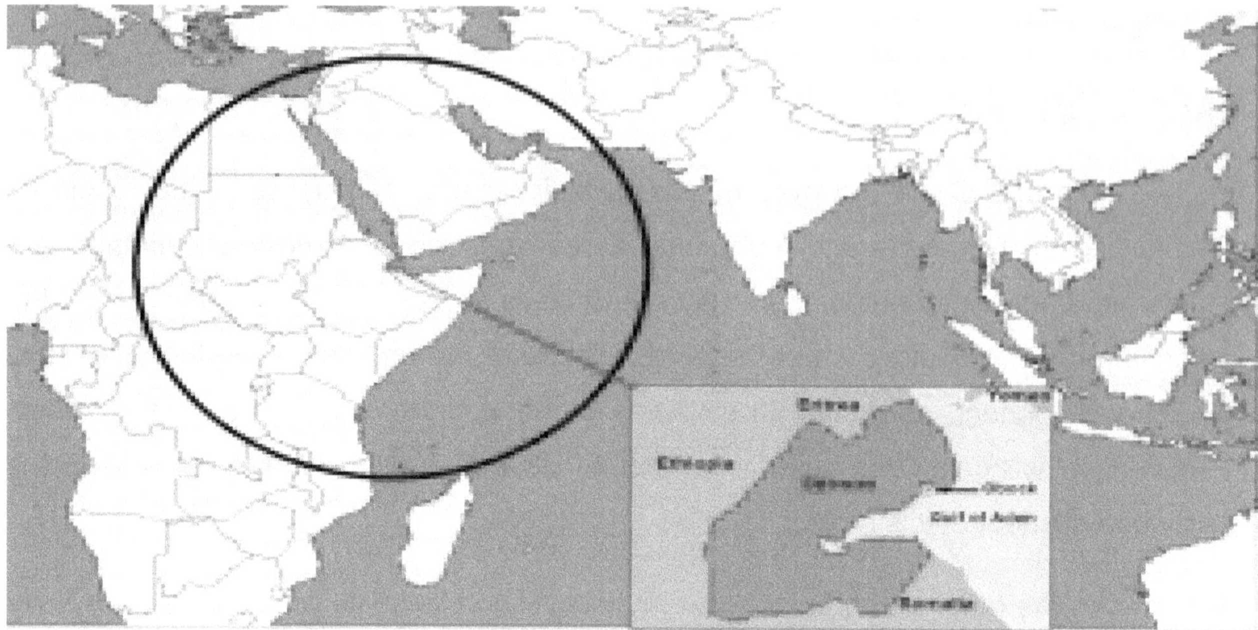

More such outposts could emerge in Pakistan, Cambodia and Myanmar in the future. China and Pakistan have conducted the sixth edition of 'the Sea Guardians' naval exercises in the Arabian Sea in January 2020. So China is trying its best to not only invest in the world but secure its investments through bilateral agreements.

Indian Dominance under threat in Ocean and Naval Expansions of India

The Indian Navy is in the phase of constant expansion. They are proposing to induct their third Aircraft carrier in the Navy. Indian Navy is already using Aircraft carrier INS Vikramaditya, while the second, INS Vikrant, is under construction in Cochin, due for commissioning in 2022. Although right now Indian Navy is operating one Aircraft carrier. These two above-mentioned naval vessels are of weight 45,000 tons each. Although a proposal is sent to the Indian CDS Gen Rawat believes that the navy would be given submarines and air-strips on far-flung Indian islands in the Indian Ocean, especially in Andaman.

INS Vikramaditya

But the Indian military expansions are not an easy task because the shared defence budget of the Indian Navy has shrunk from 18 per cent in 2013 to 13 per cent in 2019-20. Due to the fund crunch, the requirement of 200 ships has been brought down to 175. Due to this shrinking defence budgets, the Indian Navy is in hot waters and they are unable to keep an eye on the Strait of Malacca from their Andaman and Nicobar Islands. Currently, India only has 17 submarines located at Mumbai, Kochi, Visakhapatnam and Port Blair. Andaman Islands

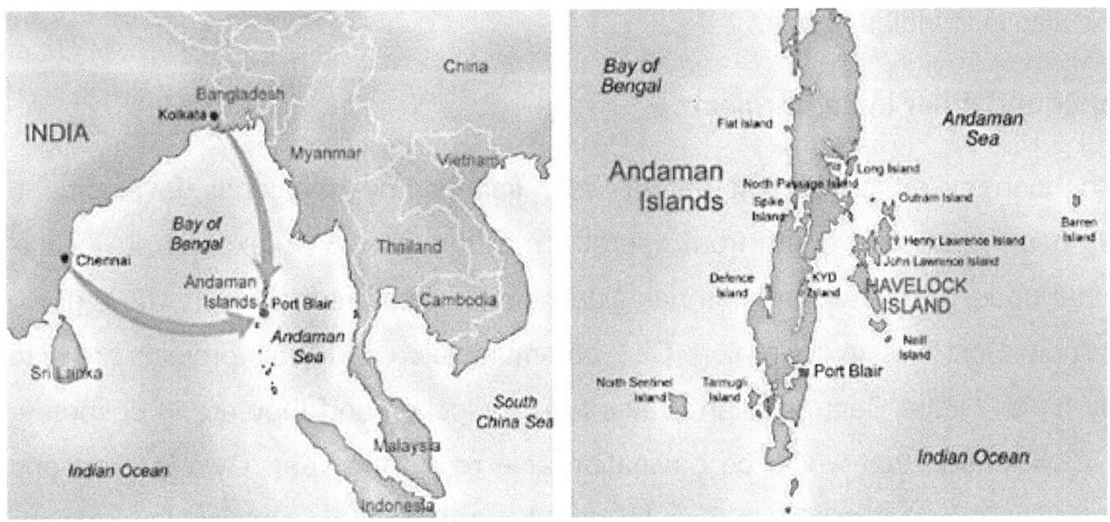

There are many wrong perceptions about China at present in Indian strategists' minds. They think that the expanding influence of China in the Indian Ocean will decrease their influence in the region. On the other hand, China wants to protect its multi-billion BRI project. Here I would like to share a maxim of Deng Xiaoping that getting rich is glorious. So China is getting glory through trade and investments but India is planning to control and monitor the Indian Ocean through its naval fleet. This Indian role is being supported by the western powers to curtail the influence of China in the region.

BRI Project

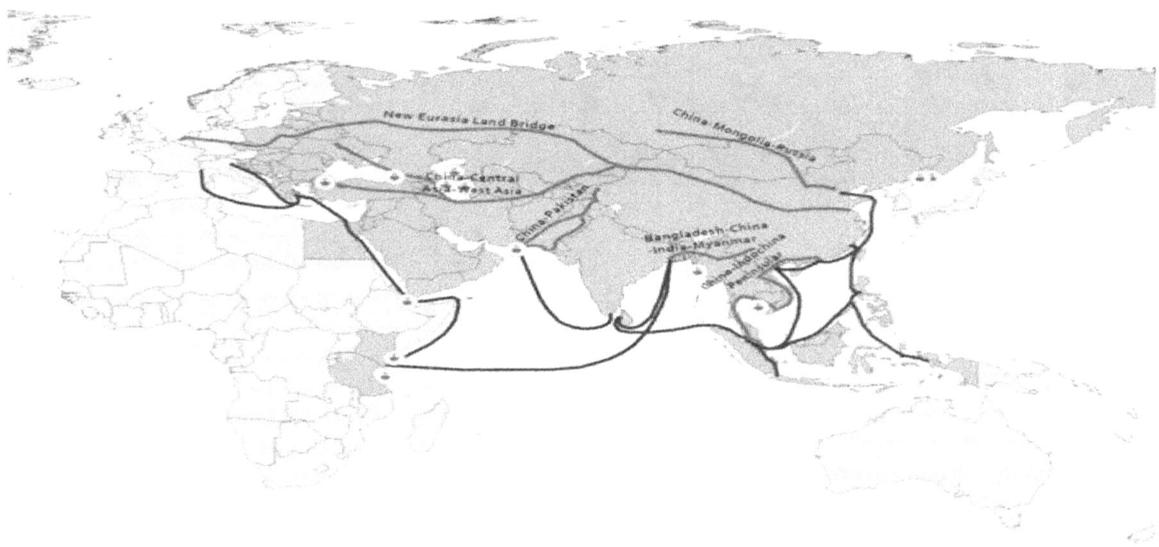

China wants to secure hits BRI project and China don't want to see the control of the Strait of Malacca in Indian hands.

Chahbahar and other Indian Projects

Chahbahar is an Iranian port that has been financed by India for its development. India has been sidelined by Iran from operations of this port. Few experts are of this opinion that under US influence India has sidelined itself from this projects.US is going to start a new 'Cold War' in the region. Gas, communication and Train projects are also halted by India. All the Central Asian States are landlocked and they are in desperate need of a warm port that would be navigation able round the year. Gwadar Port and Port Qasim can play this role even Gwadar port it is providing the shortest land access to the warm waters. In future, Pakistan and Iranian ports i.e. Chahbahar, Gwadar and Port Abbas can also be added for trade with China.

Chahbahar

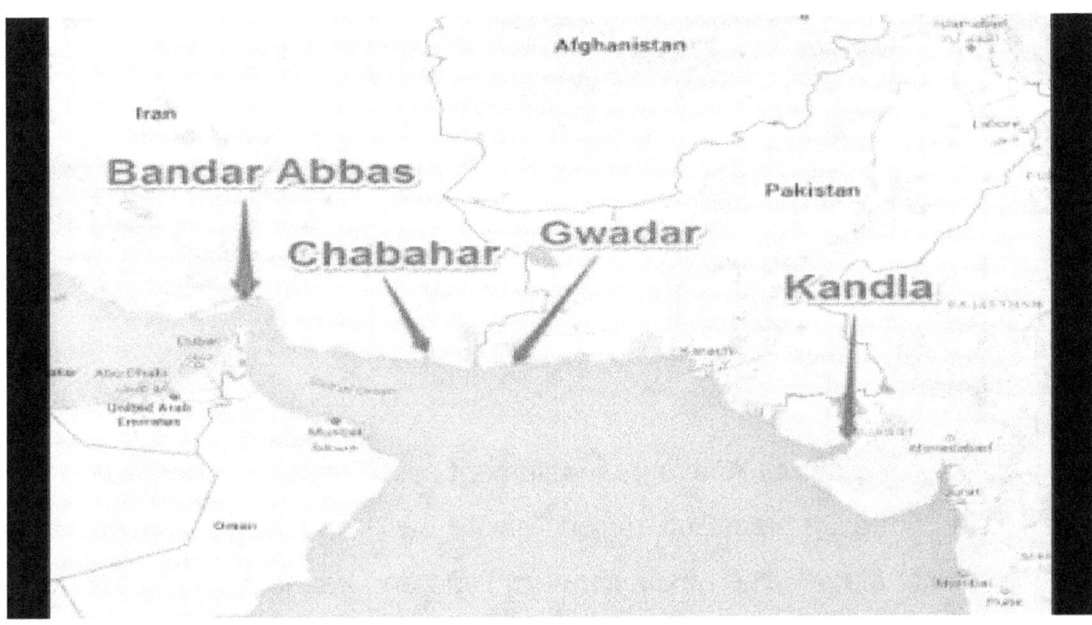

China is the main trade partner of Central Asian countries and it is exploiting the hydro-carbon of this region. The oil and gas-rich countries like Kazakhstan and Turkmenistan can fulfil the energy needs of China India and Pakistan although TAPI and CASA agreements were signed long ago they are still not materialized. Now, this is the time when we are to revive these projects. The major fields of cooperation can be energy, telecommunications, information, environmental protection and the optimum utilization of natural resources. India and Iran are cooperating on different economic and strategic fronts. These projects include Gas pipeline, Chahbahar Port, railways, trade tourism and counter-insurgency cooperation. India is planning to contain the CPEC of Pakistan by making investments in Iran and Afghanistan through different ports, power projects, trade projects and water projects.

Indian influence inside Iran is decreasing due to many reasons, according to the 'Dawn' Newspaper, After being "dropped" from a key rail project in southeastern Iran along the border with Afghanistan, India is also set to lose an ambitious gas field project in the country that had been in the pipeline for past 10 years.

Farzad-B Gas Field

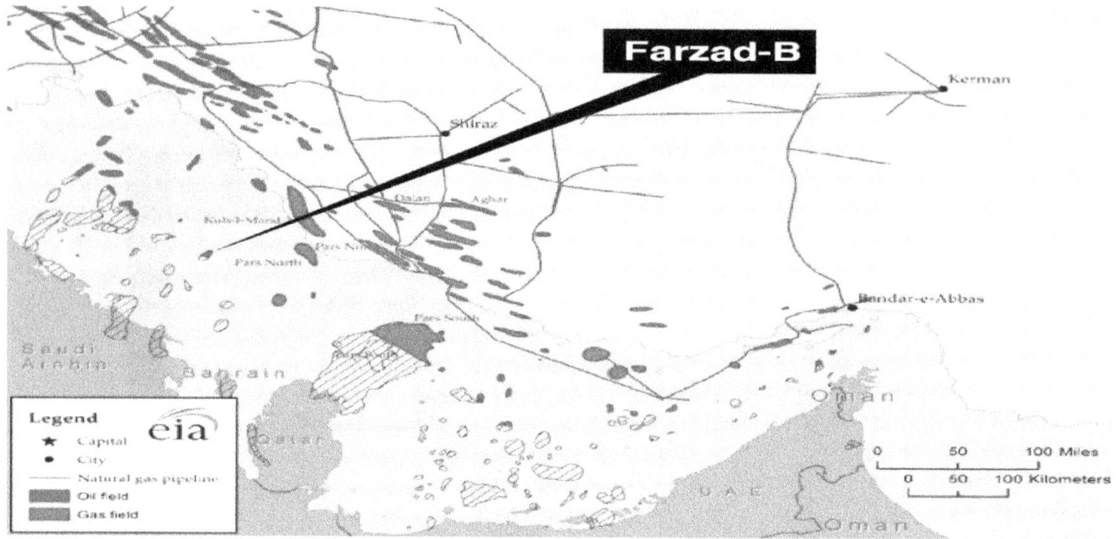

India's Ministry of External Affairs in a statement said Tehran would develop the Farzad-B gas field in the Persian Gulf region "on its own" and might engage India "appropriately at a later stage". The nexus between India and Iran is breaking and their areas of cooperation against China and Pakistan in Afghanistan is changing in the favour of Pakistan.

Geo-Strategic/Political Relations of India

China and its BRI project can be a game-changer for the region and now according to the latest news, Iran has joined it and initially US $ 400 Billion agreements are marked for investment. Right now the game between China and India is a 'zero-sum game' and the gains of India are the losses for China and vice versa. The political and geostrategic relations between the two countries are also disturbed due to the Indian attitude and China has strong reservations against Indian repealing the special status of Kashmir.

India is thinking strategically but China has set its economic agenda in mind, and all the other priorities like the South China Sea, Taiwan, disputes with India are been managed diplomatically. The strategic thinking of China by setting its goal through economic diplomacy and securing its Sea Lines of Communication (SLOC) through trade has deep-rooted effects on world trade. India has extended the role of its navy from a regional player to an international player by joining hands with other countries. India has jointly exercised with South Africa and Brazil in 'IBSAMAR' exercises. Indian Navy jointly exercised in the Indian Ocean with US and Japan named 'Malabar' started in 2002 and the last exercise was held in 2019. Australia, Bangladesh, Cambodia, Indonesia, Kenya, Malaysia, Mauritius, Myanmar, New Zealand, Oman, Seychelles, Singapore, Tanzania, Sri Lanka, Thailand, Vietnam participated in the 2018 'Milan' exercise. 'SIMBEX' exercise with Singapore and 'SLINEX' exercise with Sri Lanka were jointly exercised in the Indian Ocean. All this show of force is there to extend Indian Navy rule as blue water Navy.

Conclusion

China and India are the two mammoth players of the region. The relations between the two countries are not always cordial especially after the demise of Nehru, the bridge between these two countries has been widened. In 1962 China fought a war with India. Now China is utilizing economics diplomacy for gaining influence in the region and engaging all its opponents i.e. Japan, Taiwan and India in trade and economic war. China and India are trying to increase their sphere of influence in the region; the Indian Ocean, South China Sea, Iran and Trade are the main battlegrounds between these rivals. The rise of China is very peaceful and without fighting they are subduing their enemy. They have taken control of Hong Kong and Macao with a peaceful transition. They are engaging Taiwan in trade and the volume of their trade is more than the US $ 180 billion, with a firm policy of 'One China. The Indian ambitious rather we can say hostile posture to increase their sphere of influence by perceiving this threat that China is its enemy No one will have a deleterious effect on the regional peace. The Chinese gains are ever-increasing and Indian gains are decreasing. Its recent example is Iran where India has lost many projects including the operational control of Chahbahar port. The threat perception of India to counter Chinese influence in the region a futile effort and it will create many problems for India shortly.

The Genesis of GATT into WTO and China

Background

At the end of WWII, a new international system emerged in the world. This new political and financial system was under the control of the western world especially the United States of America became the leader of this system where different financial institutions and political organizations were established.

Britton Wood Financial System

At the end of the WWII, USA and USSR emerged as the two superpowers of the world. Both these superpowers were allies in WWII but at the end of the war, both powers became sceptical about one another. The USA worked on the new international system where United Nations was established and Britton Wood financial system was devised. Under this system, World Bank and IMF were established. This financial system is called the Britton Wood system. Initially, International Trade Organization (ITO) was negotiated but it was not ratified by the US congress. This system was fully controlled by the USA and Western Europe and the Russian and Chinese have no stakes in it.

Establishment of the GATT

For the promotion of the international trade and business General Agreement of Tariff and Trade (GATT) was signed in 1947 and ratified in 1948. The main purpose of this agreement is to promote trade and business internationally but cutting down the tariff and non-tariff barriers. The abolition of the quota system and protection policies of the governments was the main target of GATT, where systematic and gradual taxation was reduced on the products. It also enhanced the capacity of the weaker states and changed them into competitive trade markets. From 1948 till 1995 there were nine major rounds of dialogues to enhance the effectiveness of the GATT. After the Uruguay round of agreements, WTO was established in place of GATT.

What is GATT?

The General Agreement on Tariffs and Trade is a multi-national trade treaty. It has been updated in a series of global trade negotiations consisting of nine rounds between 1947 and 1995. Initially, 23 states signed an agreement in October 1947 and came into force from 01 January 1948. English and French were the official languages of the GATT. WTO was established with the signatures of 123 states in1994. The GATT, and its successor the WTO, have succeeded in reducing tariffs. The average tariff levels for the major GATT participants were reduced to many folds.

Genesis of GATT

GATT was an agreement that evolved gradually. The first round of negotiation was started in Geneva in1947 with 23 participating states.

(a) **Geneva Round** In this round 23 countries participated and almost US $ 10 billion tariff barriers were removed. It lasted for seven months

(b) **Annecy Round** France was the place where this round was hosted. It took five months to conclude this round. 34 states participated in this round.

(c) **Torquay Round** In 1950 this round took place in England where 34 states participated. After the lengthy discussions of eight months 25 % tariff was reduced by the negotiating states.

(d) **Geneva Round** Again US $ 25 billion tariffs were reduced by the discussions. In this round 22 states participated. First time Japan also joined the negotiations.

(e) **Dillon Round** Tariff concessions worth $4.9 billion of world trade was the outcome of this round of discussions. Around 45 countries participated in this round which was taken place in the Swiss city of Dillon

(f) **Kennedy Round** Again this round was taken place in a Swiss city where Tariff concessions worth $40 billion of world trade were negotiated in this round. 48 countries participated in this round of dialogues.

(g) **Tokyo Round** This round was the biggest success story for the GATT where the US $ 300 billion tariff reduction was achieved after the dialogue among the participants of around 102 countries.

(h) **Uruguay Round** Uruguay was the ninth and last round of the GATT discussions. It lasted for 87 months whereas 123 countries participated in it. Many subsidies were achieved by this round where 40 % of the overall tariff reduction was achieved.

The emergence of WTO and Chinese Entry

At the end of the last Uruguay round of discussion, it was concluded that a new setup under the name of the World Trade Organization (WTO) should have been established. 76 GATT members and the European communities were the founding members of this organization. WTO is an international organization with its headquarters and staff, and its scope includes both traded goods and trade within the service sector and intellectual property rights. In 2001 China was entered into WTO as a member. Under USA pressure China was taken as a Non-market Economy (NME) for the period of 15 years which has already been completed in 2016.

Conclusion

The establishment of the GATT and later on its conversion into WTO has created tremendous effects on the world trade and trade liberalizations. The principal of the most favoured nations has reduced many hostilities among the hostile nations. It reduces the likelihood of war and improves communications. It is considered as the enemy of the local industry, which would be under protection by the state. The international competition will replace the small cottage and struggling industry if it is not protected by the state. Overall the world is feeling the blessings of the WTO. Now China is a member of WTO and the USA is also its member. So overall, GATT was a blessing for world trade. This has open new doors of cooperation between different countries especially the hostile countries i.e. China and the USA.

South Asia

China Pakistan Economic Corridor (CPES) and Its Possible Challenges

Introduction

To analyze things from a clear and correct perspective is a great gift. The relations between India and Pakistan are a clear example of it. India is the most irritating single element in the foreign relations of Pakistan and the game between India and Pakistan is a 'zero-sum game' although the succeeding Pakistani regimes including Military Junta tried their best to change the wrong perceptions of India against Pakistan they failed. China and its ever-increasing economic might have changed the dynamics of world politics. Pak-china economic corridor constitutes one of the largest Chinese investments of $ 62 billion made under the banner of the 'One road one belt' initiative. Pakistan has increased its international posture after securing this huge investment. The CPEC will pass from the region of Jammu and Kashmir which is the constant souring point between India and Pakistan since 1947.

What is CPEC?

CPEC is the "New Silk Road" (one road) running through Central and South Asia with efforts to create a "Maritime Silk Road" (one belt) in the Indian Ocean. The two routes are to meet in the Pakistani port city of Gawadar in the Baluchistan Province, the development of which China has been promoting for many years. Upon completion, CPEC will form a network of roads, railways and gas pipelines encompassing approximately 3,000 kilometers in length. Around $11 billion is currently earmarked for infrastructure measures. The bulk of the funding, however, about $33 billion, is slated for energy projects. The aim here is to alleviate chronic energy shortages, stimulate economic development and establish new industrial parks.

Indian Reservations

India is an archrival of Pakistan and any opportunity for Pakistan is consider a loss for India and India uses such plans to restrict strategic space for Pakistan. During his visit to Iran on 23, May 2016 Prime Minister Modi signed 12 agreements with them. A trilateral agreement (including Afghanistan) for the construction of Chahbahar was also signed worth$500 million to reduce their dependency on Pakistan. The ongoing China Pakistan Economic Corridor (CPEC) project is considered to be a game-changer for the region. The corridor will not only connect the Gawadar port to Xinjiang, but it will also reduce geographical distances. Successful completion of the project will lead Pakistan towards prosperity and help it become economically strong. Indian trade with Europe, the Commonwealth of Independent States (CIS), Iran, Afghanistan and Pakistan is likely to cross the $ 500 Billion mark in the next ten years. If only 20 % of Indian trade passes through Pakistan, it is likely to stager around $ 100 Billion annually, so Indian fears have no grounds even Pakistan can earn from India by attracting them and this trade can be used as a pressure lever for India to soften its Kashmir policy.

Challenges for Pakistan

The agreements are just the kick-starters, the real challenges are lying ahead after the CPEC completion phase the challenges are infrastructure development, security, skill enhancement, Transportation Challenges, Diplomatic Balance etc. Let us discuss infrastructure development.

(a) Infrastructure Development

The Completion of China Pakistan Economic Corridor (CPEC) is expected to reduce the travel distance by 50 % for more than 33% of China's current container traffic directed towards Europe, the Middle East and Africa 70 million containers with Europe alone trade estimated over USD 1 Trillion. China produces 220 million containers annually. The share of Pakistan is 10-15 % Chinese trade would however depend upon its handling of the trade goods. The main focus of Pakistan should be to develop its Rail, Road Sea and Air travel infrastructure to cover the huge bulk of Container and other auxiliary transport. This is the weakest area of Pakistan because we are to enhance our capacity in this area to attract million-dollar container traffic. Infrastructure buildups, capacity enhancement of drivers, strong communication and road safety infrastructure is needed to be developed.

(b) Security

The security of the route is the main challenge for a country like Pakistan who is facing an insurgency in Baluchistan, War against Terrorism in KPK, urban warfare in Karachi and sectarian militancy in south Punjab. Chinese thought to first try the existing safe Eastern route but due to the political pressure of the regional parties, the toughest route was selected to execute first. The military has taken over the security and a special force is in the making to permanently look after the security for this purpose 10,000 SSD has been established for the protection of the Chinese.

(c) Skill Enhancement

Pakistan is a market of 220 million people. On the one hand, it needs the energy to meet its industrial growth and for it, there is a need for skills enhancement of manpower to cover the huge flux of investment in the sector of transportation and energy while on the other it produces top quality food items, best fruits, sports items, medical instruments, textile, leather goods, cement etc. The necessary thing is the education and skill enhancement of the workforce and entrepreneurs.

(d) Transportation Challenges

Xinjiang region is responsible for 80 % of China's total trade with Central Asia. Sea route via the Asia Pacific to Europe costs around $167 per ton and takes around 45 days; the Eurasian land bridge is likely to cut transport time by more than half and would cost $110 per ton. Travel distance would be reduced from around 26000 km to 6379 km. To avail this opportunity there is a need of linking Xinjiang with Gawadar through high-speed rail and road infrastructure.

(e) Diplomatic Balance

We are to maintain the balance between the USA and China because although China is the biggest rival of the USA it is also the biggest trade partner of the USA. After securing SCO membership now Pakistan should have pragmatic relations with Russia because Russia is not only vetoing power but it can fulfil many requirements of the military hardware for Pakistan. Gawadar is not a military outpost of China; misperceptions be cleared loudly and squarely. It is a mutual economic cooperation venture; FDI from other countries like Oman, UAE, Turkey, etc., be encouraged as it would help in clearing misperceptions as well as creating a healthy competitive environment.

Conclusion

Pakistan offers the shortest land route to central Asia for access to the Arabian Sea for their trade: 1900 km via Afghanistan as compared to Iran 2200 km or Turkey 5000 km. Moreover, CPEC further extended to, Kyrgyzstan Tajikistan, and Uzbekistan Kazakhstan offers yet another attractive option bypassing Afghanistan. So the future of Pakistan is in the timely completion of the CPEC and the stability in the region. India can be tamed by giving a lucrative share in CPEC and land access to Afghanistan but keeping Kashmir in mind. The responsibility lies on the future governments of Pakistan to actively utilize this project for the betterment of Pakistan. The role of the defence forces is also very crucial and Army is paying the role of custodian of this project. This project will be the fate changer for Pakistan and in the coming decades, Pakistan will become the mini economic power of the world.

National Internal Security Policy of Pakistan (NISP)

Introduction

The national internal security policy was presented in 2018 and is covering the period of 2018-23. It replaces the first NISP announced in 2014. It was rendered largely inconsequential by the National Action Plan produced later that year. This plan was presented on the last day by the previous government. The NISP discussed achievements made in the given era, future security challenges and proposed various recommendations on how to deal with them. According to this report, the top threats to Pakistani national security are the Tehreek-Taliban-Pakistan (TTP), Islamic State's (IS) presence in Afghanistan and possible spillover in Pakistan, return of militants from Syria and Iraq, violent extremism in educational institutions and cyber-attacks.

What is NISP and its key features?

Pakistan joined the war against terrorism after 9/11. It was a destructive phase for Pakistan and they lost 75000 people along with accumulative losses of US $ 170 Billion. Pakistan presented 1st NISP in 2014 but the complete plan was presented in the 2nd NISP in 2018. Pakistan is facing many problems and there is a long list of them. These problems are causing many problems for Pakistan; few are highlighted in 2018 NISP. The 2018 report also identifies; youth alienation and frustration, exclusionary identity narratives, lack of social justice and the rule of law, regional disparities and lack of accountability as the significant drivers of insecurity in Pakistan. So up till now, it is the most comprehensive plan to eliminate terrorism from Pakistan.

Terrorism was at its peak in the years 2008 to 2014. What contributions were made which have contributed to the decline of terrorism from its peak in 2014. The efforts include military operations like Zarb-e-Azb and Radd-ul-Fasaad, intelligence-based operations, military courts, revitalization of National Counter Terrorism Authority (NACTA) as the strategic coordinating body, creation of dedicated counter-terrorism forces in all federating units, curbing of hate speech at public places etc. In terms of choking terror financing, the National Task Force on Combating Financing of Terrorism (NTFCFT), a coordinating body of over 20 federal and provincial organizations, was established. As of March this year, sixty-six outfits were proscribed with almost 8,000 individuals placed under watch. The geo-mapping of more than 90 per cent of total religious seminaries in the country has been completed.

As compared to NISP 2014, the new policy is broader in nature. The policy outlines many strategic goals and objectives such as establishing a rule of law, creation of a shared vision, ensuring social justice and political stability.

NISP and Energy Security

The new policy focuses on three main domains Administrative, Ideational and Socio-Economic. For the administrative domain, the policy demands further enhancing the capacity, coordination and strategic planning between law enforcement agencies and government departments to deal with non-traditional threats. The policy challenges the ideological underpinnings of the extremist narrative through the ideational domain. Addressing deprivations that create breeding grounds for security challenges will be part of the socio-economic domain.

What is A6Rs?

In order to focus on these domains, A6Rs framework has been recommended. The 6Rs comprise; the Reorientation of the security apparatus by improving strategic cooperation and coordination. Reimagining the society; as a tolerant, inclusive and democratic polity by formulating a national narrative, educational and media reforms, and increasing tourism and cultural activities. The reconciliation process will begin in areas affected by militancy through re-integrating and uplifting of Khyber Pakhtunkhwa, Karachi and Balochistan. Redistributive measures focusing on the provision of social safety nets should be the focus. Moreover, it states that safety nets should be expanded for the most vulnerable sections of the society and less-privileged and underdeveloped areas should be prioritized for development. The new NISP was not divided into soft and hard components rather it was dealing with the problem as a whole while focusing on the new strategy.

To sum up, the policy has been drafted at the right time and will provide a framework to incoming federal and provincial governments on how to deal with future security challenges. The success of the policy will depend on its implementation. However, the policy needs to be further developed in the next few years with more elaboration on each strategic objective. Social justice has been set as a fourth target in the plan to eliminate terrorism and energy security is necessary to make the country invincible and independent.

Conclusion

Pakistan government has decided that they will continue to work with the global community to ensure peace and stability. NISP has implemented to achieve the common objectives of eliminating terrorism and ensuring regional peace. Due to this plan when there were 1816 incidents of terrorism in 2014, there has been a steep decline in these since. 66 organizations were proscribed with 7,966 individuals placed under watch as of March 2018. Over 90 per cent of geo-mapping of Madaris has been completed as of present. Over 1.38 million Afghan refugees have been registered under the Tripartite Agreement for Voluntary Repatriation, the most extensive voluntary repatriation programme recorded by the UNHCR. The new NISP has the ingredients to be useful. But its success depends on how seriously those entrusted with its implementation take it. The acts of terrorism have raised many international security concerns about the weak Pakistani governments and their short-sightedness has created many international and regional issues. The weakness to curb terrorism has created security issues in Central Asia Xinjiang and Afghanistan. Now the International community can hope that this plan will work successfully to curb the menace of terrorism.

Indo-Iran Relations and Pakistan

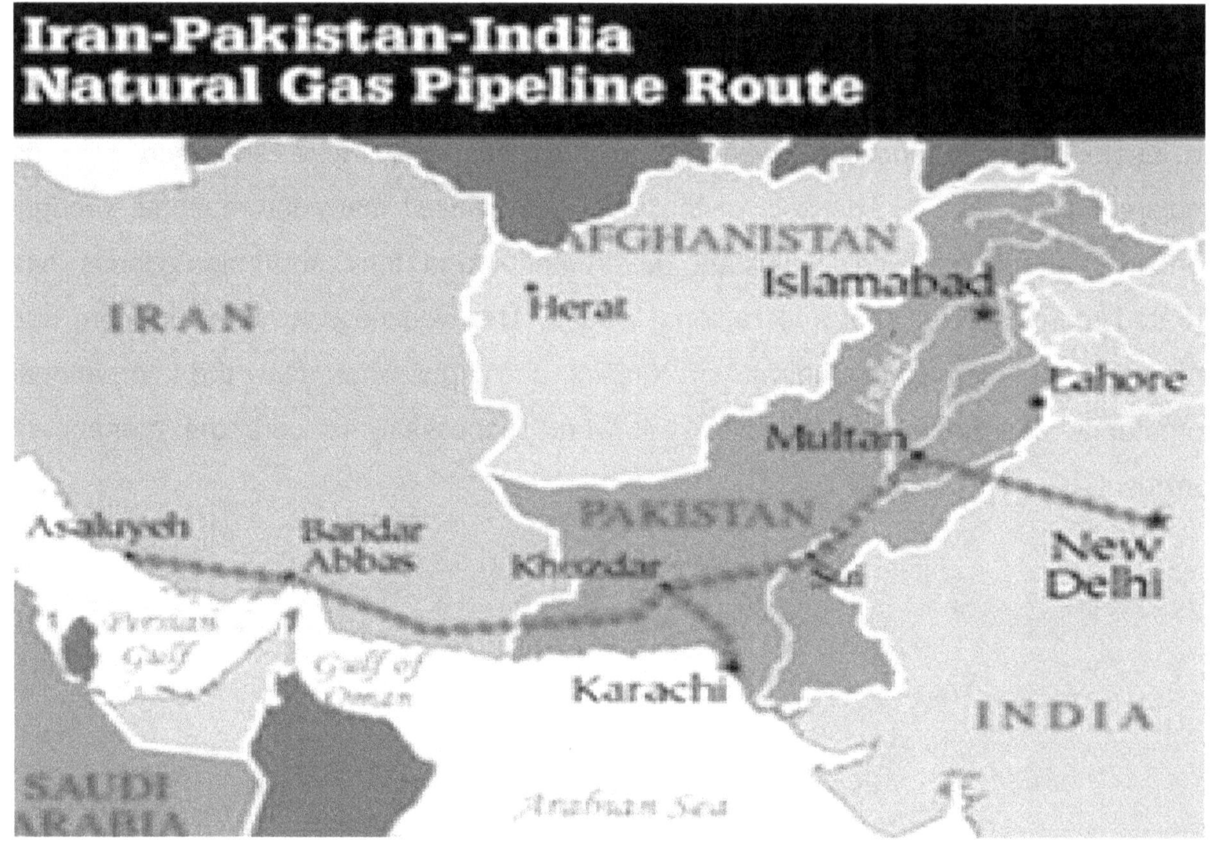

Introduction

India and Iran are the regional partners in trade and different development projects are being jointly financed and operated by these two countries. The nexus between these two countries is deep-rooted in animosity against Pakistan and they have a common approach towards different regional issues i.e. Afghanistan, energy and terrorism. Afghanistan is the common meeting point between India and Afghanistan. Pakistan and Iran enjoy a strong bond of religious, lingual and cultural bond. By setting aside these few issues, there are many common meeting points between two countries Iran historically supported Pakistan in the 1965 and 1971 war.

Background

After 14, Aug 1947 Iran was the first Muslim state who recognized Pakistan and stands with Pakistan through thick and thin. The formal relations between the two countries were established in 1948 when Liaqat Ali Khan was PM of Pakistan. Shah of Iran visited Pakistan in 1950. In 1979 regime was overthrown by Imam Khomeini's followers and the Islamic government was established in Tehran. From that time the foreign policy of Iran started working on a staunch nationalistic footing; they fought a war with Iraq and supported insurgency in Saudi Arabia. Even Pakistan felt the shock wave of sectarian violence inside Pakistan due to the Iranian support. When the Taliban came into power in Afghanistan, they were being supported by Pakistan and Iran was operating its proxies through Northern Alliance. The role of Pakistan after 9/11 decreased the policy options for Iran with Pakistan. All these successive events lead to the bridging of the gap between Iran and India and they rigorously made efforts to explore the new areas of cooperation by sidelining Pakistan.

Indo-Iran Nexus and its implications

India and Iran are cooperating on different economic and strategic fronts. These projects include Gas pipeline, Chahbahar Port, railways, trade tourism and counter-insurgency cooperation. India is planning to contain the CPEC of Pakistan by making investments in Iran and Afghanistan through different power projects, ports, trade and water projects. But this nexus is also waning due to many regional and international factors.

Indian influence inside Iran is decreasing due to many reasons. India is also set to lose an ambitious gas field project in the country that had been in the pipeline for the past 10 years. India's Ministry of External Affairs in a statement said Tehran would develop the Farzad-B gas field in the Persian Gulf region "on its own" and might engage India "appropriately at a later stage". The nexus between India and Iran is breaking and their areas of cooperation against Pakistan in Afghanistan, Baluchistan and terrorism are changing into the area of divergence between these countries.

Policy option for Pakistan

Pakistan is facing a shortage in the energy sector and Iran has ample hydro-carbon energy resources. Pakistan, a country of 220 million people with a per capita income of $1,480, is a developing economy with a GDP of $280 billion and an estimated real growth rate of 5.8 % (2018) and 3.3% (2019). Pakistan has to strengthen its trade relations with Iran and vice versa for a prosperous future. To that end, both states have to utilize economic means as well, an element of soft power, to further deepen the economic dependency for development and growth. Pakistan can rely on Iran for fulfilling the energy needs. Both countries can easily set aside India and its influence from the region by promoting trade and enhancing the level of trust between Muslim brother countries.

China and its BRI project can be a game-changer for the region and now according to the latest news, Iran has joined it and initially US $ 400 Billion agreements are marked for investment. Pakistan can take this option to establish a 'win-win game' with Iran and mark different areas of cooperation. Few areas of cooperation between these two countries are as under:

- Iran – Pakistan Gas Pipeline
- Trade: Iran – Pakistan Economic Corridor
- CPEC
- Pakistan – Iran cooperation and collaboration in Afghanistan
- Combating terrorism, extremism, & separatism
- Countering Epidemic Disease
- Energy Sector
- Counter border Corruption
- Controlling illegal goods and human trafficking
- Promotion of religious Tourism
- Gwadar – Chabhar Junction
- Marine Investment
- Defence/Military Relations
- Vocational/Professional training

> Joint working groups on regional strategic stability

Conclusion

At this moment when the global economy is on a gamble in post corona outbreak, Iran being affected by this terrible news too needs to secure its economic interests. There is likely a chance that conservative would act in a liberal and quite understanding manner when it comes to dealing with Pakistan.

Both the countries enjoyed cordial relations until 1996 but then due to divergence of interest in Afghanistan both moved apart. Pakistan was pro-Taliban whereas Iran supported the anti-Taliban alliance. India is playing with the fire in the region by investing in the hydro projects inside Afghanistan and Iran to cut the water supply to Pakistan and to cut its trade route of CPEC. Pakistan's post 9/11 policy had further increased the void. Islamabad's pro-Saudi and West policy added salt to the recipe. Being a partner of the United States of America in the war against terror, Pakistan and Iranian relations suffered a lot. However, the land connection between the two allowed reviving the relationship while the trade routes of CPEC can be extended to Iran and India should be isolated by positively engaging Iran in trade and energy projects. Indian dream of becoming a regional power will be shattered by actively utilizing the diplomatic corps and foreign missions by Pakistan.

International Law and the Settlement of Indo-Pak Territorial Disputes

Introduction

International law is not binding law but the signatory state is responsible to abide by its clauses. Indo-Pak disputes i.e. Kashmir, Siachin, Sir Creek and water disputes can be amicably resolved through international laws. The presence of international bodies like UNSC, UN, WB and IMF has a very decisive say in world issues. Pakistan and India had resolved their water dispute through the mediation of the World Bank. UN has resolutions about Kashmir.

Origin of International Law

According to the Encyclopedia Britannica International law reflects the establishment and subsequent modification of a world system founded almost exclusively on the notion that independent sovereign states are the only relevant actors in the international system. The essential structure of international law was mapped out during the European Renaissance, though its origins lay deep in history and can be traced to cooperative agreements between peoples in the ancient Middle East. International Law is also called the Public international law or the law of nations.

International Law and Peaceful Settlements of Disputes

Peaceful settlement of international disputes is a fundamental principle of international law of a peremptory character. It is formulated as such in the UN Charter (Article 2.3) and developed in UNGA Resolution 2625 on Principles of International Law concerning friendly relations and co-operation among states. The origins of this principle can be traced back to the first Hague Peace Conference in 1899, which produced a Convention for the Pacific Settlement of International Disputes. The Second Hague Peace Conference, in 1907, yielded another Convention for the Pacific Settlement of International Disputes. Within the League of Nations' Covenant, this commitment to pacific dispute settlement was reinforced by a moratorium on the use of force. The states' obligation to resolve their differences by pacific methods gained all its significance when the prohibition of the use of force was eventually formulated in article 2.4 of the United Nations Charter.

Short HIstory of International Law

Historically, International Law has been regarded by the international community as a means to ensure the establishment and preservation of world peace and security. The maintenance of international peace and security has always been the major purpose of International Law. It was the basic objective behind the creation of the League of Nations in 1919 and the United Nations in 1945. Since the direct cause of war and violence is always a dispute between States, it is therefore in the interest of peace and security that disputes should be settled. Methods and procedures for the pacific settlement of disputes have been made available in International Law.

Scope of International Law

All regional and international conflicts came under the jurisdiction of International Humanitarian Law. Article 3 common to all four Geneva Conventions represent the first attempt to lay down rules governing non-international armed conflicts. It has been described as a "convention in miniature" because it contains within it the basic minimum standards of international humanitarian law applicable in conflict situations. The International Court of Justice reinforced this view, stating that the rules in common Article 3 reflect elementary considerations of humanity applicable under customary international law to any armed conflict. Pakistan and India are hostile states and they are perpetual enemies of each other. Pakistan is always of this opinion that international powers have to interfere to resolve the core issues between India and Pakistan on the other hand India is of this opinion that all the issues between two countries should be resolved through bilateral dialogues as per the Shimla Agreement.

Guarantees in International Laws

All persons not directly participating in the conflict or who have ceased to do so because, for example, they are hors de combat or have surrendered are entitled to be treated humanely and to receive respect for their person, religious practices, honour and convictions without adverse distinction. Under Protocol II it is prohibited to order that there will be no survivors Besides, Protocol II contains a catalogue of fundamental guarantees prohibiting at anytime and anywhere:

- Violence to life, health and physical or mental wellbeing of persons, in particular, murder as well as cruel treatment such as torture, mutilation or any form of corporal punishment
- Collective punishments
- Taking of hostages
- Acts of terrorism
- Outrages upon personal dignity, in particular humiliating and degrading treatment, rape, enforced prostitution and any form of indecent assault
- Slavery and the slave trade in all their forms

- ➢ Pillage
- ➢ Threats to commit any of the foregoing acts

The international law provides protection and guarantees for the safeguarding of the children, women, detainees etc. the following protections are given to them. Children less than 15 years are exempted to take part in armed conflicts; Women are made protected from forced labour and sex. Detainees and POWs are to be treated as per IHL, the fair trial has been guaranteed, general amnesty has been encouraged, human life is very vital to protect so medical treatment is guaranteed to all, all types of civil population is protected from mass bombing etc. So this humanitarian law covers all the eventualities in the case of possible provocations between India and Pakistan.

Conclusion

There are many conflicts taking place in the world but International Law is unable to protect the people because the powerful countries of the world have drawn different lines for them. International law provides different guarantees to the people of the world. International law allows India and Pakistan to resolve their issues through dialogue and negotiations. All the bilateral issues of India and Pakistan can be resolved through dialogue and interactions. The core issues between two nuclear belligerent states can only be resolved through composite dialogue. These dialogue can be initiated and carried out through the help of International players or bilaterally.

Diplomacy of Pakistan

Introduction

"Foreign policy cannot be reactional, incidental or occasional; clearly defined goals have to be followed with consistency to achieve tangible results."Quaid-e-Azam MA Jinnah had spelt out Pakistan's foreign policy soon after the birth of Pakistan in these words: "Our objective should be peace within and peace without. We want to live peacefully and maintain cordial and friendly relations with our immediate neighbours and with the world at large. We have no aggressive designs against anyone. We stand by the United Nations Charter and will gladly make our contribution to the peace and prosperity of the world". The Increasing globalization and new realities that are emerging on the global horizon are pushing Pakistan to refine its role in diplomacy in changing the world after 9/11.

Pakistan's diplomatic overtures

This change has been well reflected in Pakistan's policy in recent years with a focus on increasing diplomatic and high-level exchanges, enhancing trade, attracting investment and extending cooperation in many areas under the broad framework of Vision East Asia formulated in October 2003. Vision East Asia is designed to emulate the example of East Asian miracle economies in development. Pakistan decided to become the Asian tiger by strengthening its economy by implementing trade and investment-friendly policies.

9/11 and Pakistan

In the aftermath of 9/11, another international conspiracy was hatched to dismember Pakistan. This time the conspiracy was much larger in scope and more dangerous in intent. Pakistan was to be befriended and then cut into four quasi-states. In this, India is being supported by the USA, Afghanistan, Britain, Israel and the West in general. The tools in use are TTP, BLA, BRA, BLF, and segment of media bolstered by bloggers, foreign paid NGOs and international media. Daesh is the latest group added to their arsenal. The goals are to destabilize, de-Islamize, denuclearize and balkanize Pakistan using covert means and psychological operations. Pakistan was made to fight terrorism on its soil, then accused of harbouring terrorists in safe havens in FATA and aiding cross border terrorism in Afghanistan, occupied

Kashmir and India, and then constantly pressed to do more. The terrorist groups in FATA, Baluchistan were funded, equipped and trained to fight and exhaust Pakistan security forces. MQM was funded and its militants trained in India to make Karachi lawless.

Diplomatic Weaknesses

India and Afghanistan were projected as victims of terrorism and Pakistan as an incubator of terrorism. The covert war launched from Afghan soil in 2002 has incurred a loss of 70,000 fatalities, injuries to tens of thousands, destruction of property, $ 170 billion financial loss and immense social trauma. Pakistan has come under foreign debt of over \$100 billion.9/11 changed global politics and Pakistan was once again befriended by the USA and made a coalition partner to fight the global war on terror as a frontline state. Pakistan for a second time shifted all its eggs in the basket of the USA. Between 2004 and 2008, Indo-Pak relations improved as a result of a peace treaty and resumption of dialogue, giving rise to optimism that core disputes will be resolved.

(a) ISAF Role and Front Line State

Indo-US-Israel agenda of disabling Pakistan's nuclear programme or as a minimum curtailing its minimum deterrence capability remain unchanged. Afghanistan under Hamid Karzai remained aligned with India and hostile to Pakistan. Afghan Unity government under Ghani-Abdullah is far worse. NATO, USA in the guise of ISAF done nothing for Pakistan and all the terrorists were shifted inside Pakistan and we were failed to fight our case.

(b) Pak Iran Relations

Pak-Iran relations are frosty and practically, Iran is more close to India and Afghanistan. Pakistan foreign policymakers are faced with perpetually hostile India, near hostile Afghanistan, and the changed attitude of the US. Washington has callously whipped Pakistan under its 'do more' policy and is now hurling warnings. Its heavy tilt towards India is a matter of anxiety for Pakistan. Iran nurtures grouses on account of Pakistan's closeness with Saudi Arabia, and for sending Gen (R) Raheel to Riyadh to head 41-member Sunni Muslim States Alliance.

(c) Arab Spring and Diplomacy Failures

Warmth in the relationship with the GCC States has diluted because of Pakistan not agreeing to send troops to Saudi Arabia to ward off the threat from Yemen. Saudi-Qatar tiff is another challenge faced by Pakistan since it cannot afford to take sides.

(d) Unresolved Kashmir Issue

Pakistan has been deliberately kept politically unstable by making it play the game of ladder and snake so that it remains economically dependent. It was pulled down whenever it grew economically strong. That is why it has been lurching from one crisis to another in its 70 years checkered history. Kashmir was still not resolved after 70 years although we supported the USA in a war against terrorism. It is our diplomatic failure.

(e) India and Diplomacy

Pakistan is faced with multiple threats of Indo-US-Afghan covert war, India's Cold Start Doctrine, the US Af-Pak doctrine, and Hybrid war and all these threats have now become menacing. The threat to its security has heightened after the signing of three Indo-US defence agreements in 2016 and the US openly expressing its enmity against Pakistan and love for India. India is getting unnerved on account of the high-intensity freedom struggle in occupied Kashmir, which is slipping out of its hands and is endangering the unity of India. India has no other choice except to keep persecuting the Kashmiris ruthlessly, keep the LoC on fire and diplomatically place Pakistan on the back foot.

Conclusion

While many developing countries have raced ahead, Pakistan is still struggling and has neither become to make it independent of these issues. Now it is time to resolve these issues through proactive and independent diplomacy. Pakistan is a nuclear state and it was the resources to resolve the Afghanistan issue but the continuous hostility with India has deprived it of its real strength. In future, both the state can use the SCO platform to start new dialogues for the resolution of the core issues. All the issues can be resolved through positive engagement.

Core Objectives of Pakistan's Foreign Policy

Introduction

The countries and systems are run through guided principles that why the foreign policy cannot be reactionary, incidental or occasional; clearly defined goals have to be followed with consistency to achieve tangible results. The leader of the nation Quaid-e-Azam MA Jinnah had spelt out Pakistan's foreign policy soon after the birth of Pakistan in these words: "Our objective should be peace within and peace without. We want to live peacefully and maintain cordial and friendly relations with our immediate neighbours and with the world at large. We have no aggressive designs against anyone. We stand by the United Nations Charter and will gladly make our contribution to the peace and prosperity of the world ".

The foreign policy of Pakistan

This change has been well reflected in Pakistan's policy in recent years with a focus on increasing diplomatic and high-level exchanges, enhancing trade, attracting investment, and extending cooperation in many areas under the broad framework of Vision East Asia formulated in October 2003. Vision East Asia is designed to emulate the example of East Asian miracle economies in development.

Core Objectives of the Foreign Policy of Pakistan

Pakistan is facing an existential threat from the very first day of its establishment. Munir Akram (Pakistan's Ambassador in UN) said "unlike its daunting domestic objectives, Pakistan's external agenda, though challenging, is fairly clear". And, although overstretched, Islamabad has the capacity in its Foreign Service and the 'security establishment' to address this agenda. Building the Pakistan-China strategic partnership: China has the strategic motivation and financial, technological and weapons capabilities to help Pakistan emerge as a militarily strong and economically dynamic state. The substance and depth of the future strategic partnership will depend mainly on the ability of the Pakistan government and its private sector to conceive and execute cooperative projects and ventures with China. A special entity dedicated to a timely and efficient implementation of CPEC could be decisive in realizing its full potential.

Kashmir and Strategic relations with China are the main core issues in the foreign policy of Pakistan. According to the website of the Ministry Of Foreign Affairs, the objectives are as under

- ➤ Promotion of Pakistan as a dynamic, progressive, moderate, and democratic Islamic country.
- ➤ Developing friendly relations with all countries of the world, especially major powers and immediate neighbours.
- ➤ Safeguarding national security and geostrategic interests, including Kashmir.
- ➤ Consolidating our commercial and economic cooperation with the international community.
- ➤ Safeguarding the interests of Pakistani Diaspora abroad.
- ➤ Ensuring optimal utilization of national resources for regional and international cooperation.

Pakistan as a progressive country

India and Afghanistan were projected as victims of terrorism and Pakistan as an incubator of terrorism. The covert war launched from Afghan soil in 2002 has incurred a loss of 70,000 fatalities, injuries to tens of thousands, destruction of property. Between 2004 and 2008, Indo-Pak relations improved as a result of a peace treaty and resumption of dialogue, giving rise to optimism that core disputes will be resolved.

Friendly relations with all countries

Indo-US-Israel agenda of disabling Pakistan's nuclear programme or as a minimum curtailing its minimum deterrence capability remain unchanged. Afghanistan under Hamid Karzai remained aligned with India and hostile to Pakistan. Afghan Unity government under Ghani-Abdullah is far worse. NATO, USA in the guise of ISAF done nothing for Pakistan and all the terrorists were shifted inside Pakistan and we were failed to fight our case but Pakistan remained friendly.

Kashmir Issue

Pakistan has been deliberately kept politically unstable by making it play the game of ladder and snake so that it remains economically dependent. It was pulled down whenever it grew economically strong. That is why it has been lurching from one crisis to another in its 70 years checkered history. Kashmir was still not resolved after 70 years although we supported the USA in the war against terrorism. It is our diplomatic failure of Pakistan that India has revoked Article 370 of the Indian Constitution which has changed the status of Kashmir but it will not end the claim of Pakistan on this part of the land.

International cooperation

Pakistan is faced with multiple threats of Indo-US-Afghan covert war, India's Cold Start Doctrine, the US Af-Pak doctrine, and hybrid war and all these threats have now become menacing. The threat to its security has heightened after the signing of three Indo-US defence agreements in 2016 and the US openly expressing its antagonism against Pakistan and love for India. India is getting unnerved on account of the high-intensity freedom struggle in occupied Kashmir, which is slipping out of its hands and is endangering the unity of India. India has no other choice except to keep persecuting the Kashmiris ruthlessly, keep the LoC on fire and diplomatically place Pakistan on the back foot.

Conclusion

While many developing countries have raced ahead, Pakistan is still struggling and has neither become to make itself independent of these issues. Now it is time to resolve these issues amicably and have a focus on the core issues of the foreign policy. Pakistan can achieve all of its objectives through proactive and independent diplomacy revolving around the concept of regional peace and cooperation. The alliance diplomacy and the devastating policy to be a front line state have limited the scope and choices for Pakistan. Neutral and objective diplomacy can resolve many regional and international challenges for Pakistan.

Civil-Military Relations in Pakistan

Introduction

The military in Pakistan enjoys the centre of the power stage throughout its chequered history of politics and Dictatorship. Military Top brass may not be interested in gaining power but they always have powerful say in all the decision makings. Their disposition towards the civilian government is shaped primarily by their professional and corporate interests. They are prepared to work with a government as long as it can cope with the problems of governance effectively and transparently and does not threaten their interests. The civilian government enjoys sufficient freedom for political and economic management, but it has to give due consideration to the military's sensitivities and sensibilities especially in the areas of Atomic program, Foreign policy, Kashmir and Economic Agenda.

Historical Background

Historically military enjoys the most powerful role in this country like many of the African and Latin American countries. The ethnic, religious cleavages and economic mismanagement remained the topmost weaknesses of the political class in the developing countries. The cronyism, plutocracy, nepotism and lack of meritocracy have thawed the power of Politicians, contrary to that military institutions are known for their meritocracy, strategic command and will to deliver have superseded the waning power of the Political aristocracy. Ayub khan was the first military dictator who is more famous for his development model and mega projects especially the dams and industrial infrastructure, until now four Military dictators have ruled Pakistan.

Military Nature and Coups

According to Professor Campbell "The political values of Pakistan's military unlike the others in this study of Muslim world militaries are openly pro-Islamist. Its values are not as clearly defined as the secular worldviews of either Turkey or Syria, with their Ataturkist and Ba'thist ideologies respectively. The circumstances of Pakistan's birth in which Islam was used to justifying statehood and its regional competition with India and in Afghanistan, led it to support jihadists in the east and later the west are relevant to the evolution of the military's values in practical terms. That is, the military works cooperatively with Islamist groups, both political and guerrilla, or terrorist, in nature". These allegations are very severe for a nuclear-capable military.

The military was professional and secular till 1980 then it was Islamized by General Zia Like the administrations of the British, Yahya Khan and Ayub Khan, that of Zia ul-Haq believed that the 'common Pakistani' was inherently religious and used religious symbolism to help legitimize its rule. The difference between the ideological stand of Pakistan's third military regime and its predecessors is not a qualitative one. Only because Zia had to come to terms with a relatively more difficult political situation than his predecessors did he push the logic of religious manipulation to its most extreme form. Afghanistan Jihad played a major role to strengthen the grip of General Zia on power.

Fragile Political System

The fragile institutions and weaker will to govern is the main weakness that motivates the Military to protect the wider national goals and support the state for economic stability. During the martial laws, the growth rate remained on average 6% per annum. The military is the most developed organization in the country and they have good management experience. They support merit-based selection and performance. The military takeover is an open secret and according to the experts' opinion, the role of the military is ever-present in the political system of Pakistan and it is strengthening the fragile governance system of this country. No government can rule out the military from the corridors of power.

Conclusion

The political class is a fragile one on the other hand military class is also having different shades the military class is divided into four groups. According to the expert Cohen (1984), there are four generations of Pakistani officers that have influenced Pakistani politics: the British Generation, the American Generation, the Pakistani Generation 1972-82, and the Next Generation. Now it is time to end this all mess and strengthen the political institution so that can take control of the institutions and the military should perform her constitutional role because the fragile political class and weaker political system are not in the favour of stronger nuclear power in Pakistan.

Current Situation in Kashmir and Its Implications on Indian Subcontinent

Introduction

Before the partition of India, there was 565 princely states and they were independent in their internal affairs but their external affairs i.e. defence and Foreign policy were under British control. Kashmir was also a princely state before the partition. The process of partitioning British India was governed by the 1947 Indian Independence Act. Princely states were not directly incorporated in either dominion. Princely states were theoretically granted the option to stay independent or accede to either dominion. The states were encouraged by then-Viceroy Lord Mountbatten to accede to one dominion or the other and did so based on their geographical position, religious identity, or other factors. Maharaja Hari Singh was the ruler of Kashmir he was also given the same options to join one country or remain independent.

The ruler of Kashmir was Hindu Dogra but the majority of the State was Muslim by their religion. This Hindu ruler decided to join India rather than Pakistan on the condition that it was granted a level of autonomy. Over the years, that autonomy was worn down by the central state, but opposition to Kashmir's "special status" has only increased since, with the rise of Hindu nationalism. The two most significant concessions given to Kashmir in the Indian constitution of 1950 were Article 370 and Article 35A. Article 370 gave Indian-administered Kashmir autonomy in all areas except defence, communication and foreign policy. Article 35A gave only "permanent residents" of Kashmir the right to own property. Since the 1950s, Hindu nationalists have rallied against these exceptions, arguing that Hindu-majority India must not bend its constitution for Muslim-majority Kashmir. During the 2019 election campaign, the BJP promised to revoke Kashmir's "special status," tapping into many Hindu voters' hostility toward Muslims and mistrust of Pakistan.

Why is Kashmir controversial?

Kashmir is situated in Himalayas and India and Pakistan both have their claims. The area was once a princely state called Jammu and Kashmir, but it joined India in 1947 soon after the sub-continent was divided up at the end of British rule. In1948 both the Countries fought a limited war on Kashmir and the state was divided into Indian held Kashmir and Pakistan Azad Kashmir. Around 1988 the separatist movement in Indian held Kashmir started and a full-fledged separatist movement was started in Kashmir against India.

Present development in Kashmir?

It was on the agenda of the BJP to scrap the age-old special status of Kashmir under Article 370. In August 2019 there were signs of something taking place in Kashmir. Tens of thousands of additional Indian troops were deployed, a major Hindu pilgrimage was cancelled, schools and colleges were shut, tourists were ordered to leave, telephone and internet services were suspended and regional political leaders were placed under house arrest.PM Narendra Modi is a right-wing Hindu nationalist, he thought that this special status of Kashmir is against Indian nationalism. After his second term in office, there was speculation that Article 35A of the Indian constitution, which gave some special privileges to the people of the state, would be scrapped. The government then stunned everyone by saying it was revoking nearly all of Article 370, which 35A is part of and which has been the basis of Kashmir's complex relationship with India for some 70 years.

Explicit and implicit implications of this Indian action

The article allowed the state a certain amount of autonomy to Kashmir, a separate flag and freedom to make laws. Foreign affairs, defence and communications remained the preserve of the central government. As a result, Jammu and Kashmir could make their own rules relating to permanent residency, ownership of property and fundamental rights. It could also bar Indians from outside the state from purchasing property or settling there. The constitutional provision has underpinned India's often fraught relationship with Kashmir, the only Muslim-majority region to join India at partition.

Prime Minister Narendra Modi and his staunch nationalist party BJP were ever opposing these special Articles and they considered that these Articles are the factors, which are ruining the unification of India constitutionally and creating divisions. They argued it needed to be scrapped to integrate Kashmir and put it on the same footing as the rest of India. After winning the 2019 elections they were ready to scrape these special Articles. Many critics are of this opinion that due to this unhealthy and useless opening of a new front, India has made compromises on its economic growth. The ruling BJP and its right-wing allies have challenged Article 35A which it calls discriminatory, through a series of petitions. According to Shukla, "the order will face both legal and political challenges in the coming days". The first legal challenge will come from Kashmir itself. Doing away with Article 370 now opens the door for an open Palestine-type independence struggle within Kashmir," he said."In India as well, there will be mounting legal challenges and political opposition which has many illustrious lawyers. It can be expected that these will be heard by a constitutional bench in the Supreme Court."

Conclusion

There hasn't been much of a state government in Jammu and Kashmir for over a year now. Although, according to the Indian constitution only state assembly's consent is necessary for changing the status of any state. Last year Mehbooba Muft's government was reduced to a minority. This meant the federal government only had to seek the consent of the governor who imposes its rule. No opposition party will challenge this federal government decision because of the opposition by the average Indian which would consider that move as an anti-India move. The Indian government made an unconstitutional move against the will of the people of Kashmir. Pakistan and China have shown strong reservations against this move and they not only strongly condemned the move even they internationally started a diplomatic offensive against that move. The response of the international powers especially the USA and UK are very weak. This move has led to a new era of resistance and in the coming years, it will lead to many other challenges for regional peace.

Role of Think Tanks in the Making of US Foreign Policy Towards South Asia

FOREIGN AFFAIRS

published by
THE COUNCIL ON FOREIGN RELATIONS

Introduction

The USA is the sole superpower of the world after the demise of the USSR in 1991. The foreign policy of countries like the USA is based on three tiers firstly, Global secondly, regional and thirdly, bilateral. All these three levels are dealt with differently. The most importance is given to global foreign policy. Sustained bilateral and multilateral U.S. engagement in South Asia is of the essence. Three major factors amplify the importance of placing South Asia on the crowded front burner of U.S. foreign policy priorities: Threats to stability emanating from the region, the overall strategic significance of South Asia, and several notable geopolitical shifts. These shifts are the U.S. combat withdrawal from Afghanistan, an accelerating American rebalance to Asia, and resilient and expanding global terrorist networks.

At the same time, sustained engagement presents policy challenges for Washington. These include addressing definitional disagreements with India about what should constitute a strategic relationship, crafting a proper policy for engaging Bangladesh in that country's highly fraught political and security environment and identifying ways to help promote stability in two troubled countries Afghanistan and

Pakistan. Washington is likely to have a lighter footprint in the months and years ahead in these two countries.

Role of Media and Think Tanks

The role of media and think tanks is very deep-rooted in USA foreign policy. Historically they enjoy a very strong role in USA policymaking. According to the Richard N. Haass Director of Policy and Planning U.S. Department of State From the perspective of U.S. policy-makers, today's think tanks offer five principal benefits, according to Ambassador Richard N. Haass, who is Director of Policy and Planning at the State Department. He says they generate "new thinking" among U.S. decision-makers, provide experts to serve in the administration and Congress, give policy-makers a venue in which to build shared understanding on policy options, educate U.S. citizens about the world, and provide third-party mediation for parties in conflict.

After the termination of the Bretton-Woods financial system, states experienced an increasing level of transnational market interaction. This led to a consequent boost of transnational capital flows, an event that shifted control of the national economy away from the state. Governments cannot regulate the inflow and outflow of capital without interfering with the system of laissez-faire. Due to the anarchic nature of the international system, no state can successfully attain and hold the position of global hegemony. The world is too vast for any state's limited reach. Thus, a state in the pursuit of security and prosperity needs to use further means to influence other actors in the international system. Two of the main elements that will guide us through the examination of the media's effect on a state's relative level of prestige are institutional interdependence and the liberal school of thought's approach to foreign policymaking.

Continued engagement

Due to the strict policy challenges the USA is of this opinion to have a continued engagement with South Asia especially Pakistan and Afghanistan to curb terrorism and separatism which is a menace not only for the region but for the world. The panacea of world peace lies in this region.

US foreign policy towards South Asia

The foreign policy of the USA towards South Asia is very chequered and confusing. The USA projected India and Afghanistan as victims of terrorism and Pakistan as an incubator of terrorism. The covert war launched from Afghan soil in 2002 has incurred a loss of 75,000 fatalities, injuries to tens of thousands, destruction of property, $ 185 billion financial loss and immense social trauma.

Pakistan has come under foreign debt of $90 billion. 9/11 changed global politics and Pakistan was once again befriended by the USA and made a coalition partner to fight the global war on terror as a frontline state. Pakistan for a second time placed all its policy options eggs in the basket of the USA. Between 2004 and 2008, Indo-Pak relations improved as a result of a peace treaty and resumption of dialogue, giving rise to optimism that core disputes will be resolved. In the aftermath of 9/11, another international conspiracy was hatched to disjoint Pakistan. Pakistan was made to fight terrorism on its soil, then accused of harbouring terrorists in safe havens in FATA and aiding cross border terrorism in Afghanistan, occupied Kashmir and India, and then constantly pressed to do more. The terrorist groups in FATA, Baluchistan were funded, equipped and trained to fight and exhaust Pak security forces. All the foreign policy of the USA is based on the media reports and Pakistan and Afghanistan are suffering from this narrow approach of the USA.

Conclusion

Foreign policy cannot be reactional, incidental or occasional; clearly defined goals have to be followed with consistency to achieve tangible results. The USA foreign policy about South Asia is reactional, biased and narrowly designed for selective objectives. The behaviour of the USA from 1979 has seen many ups and downs after strategic policy shifts. This has badly hampered the sustainability of the issues of this region. Media and biased and conservative think tanks are continually shaping narrow agendas and the US state department is following it. The USA has to broaden its agenda for South Asia especially for Pakistan, India and Afghanistan so that it can openly be engaged with the regional countries as per the longer-term policy goals.

Russia

NATO and Russian Revival

Background

When the fog of WWII evaporated, the two Allied countries USSR and the USA were standing in the hostile camps and they were at dagger drawn. The problem of this hostility started when the Berlin city was unified by the three allied powers unilaterally without consulting the USSR. It was a big blow for the USSR. Later on, the USA and western European countries established NATO in 1949 and started the policy of containment of communism. In retaliation to these acts, USSR started the Warsaw Pact agreement in 1955. The establishment of NATO was against USSR but when it was dismembered in 1991 there was not a legal, rational, political and logical requirement of NATO.

Why NATO was established?

NATO was established to counter the threat of Russian aggression against the Western World. When it was established against the communist bloc it was a justifiable act of the USA. But in the years to come, the worth of NATO has been a decline with time. NATO jumped into the Afghanistan conflict and violated the UN mandate given to the regional organizations. After the demise of the USSR, it was estimated that NATO will be disbanded by the USA but it never happened even it was further expanded towards the Russian border.

Russian Revivalism

After the demise of the USSR in 1991, fifteen states emerged from that country. Russia was considered the successor of the USSR. When USSR was disintegrated its economy perished and Russians were queuing for one loaf of bread. Before the fall there was less disparity in the wages and only 1:8 ratios of salaries difference were there but after 1991 this gap was widened.

(a) **The emergence of Putin** President Putin jumped into the power arena in Moscow and defeated the entire powerful politician. He is the only person in Russian history that remained in power for more than twenty years in the recent past. Only Stalin can beat his record. The phenomenal rise of Putin in 1991 is the main reason for the Russian revival.

(b) **Revival as a regional power** Russia could not become a superpower in a night, so the strategists decided to opt for a regional power role. Russia expanded its influence in Central Asia, Syria, Libya Turkey and Ukraine. This gradual rise has proven that Russia is a middle-order or a regional power of the world.

(c) **Revival of the soft power** It was difficult to switch to the soft image but it was done and in the entire crisis like Corona, Wiki leaks, American Elections etc. Russian has proved their image as a leading soft power of the world.

NATO and Russian Revivalism Hegel said that there would be the antithesis of every thesis. So the revival of Russia is the antithesis of the presence of NATO in the region. NATO after negotiation admitted that they will not expand themselves to the Russian borders and but they did it.

Conclusion

NATO expanded their area and occupied the Warsaw Pact bunkers and missile launchers. The power of NATO was increased in many folds. Rose and Orange revolutions in Eastern Europe frustrated the Russians. Although the presence of NATO in Europe is not the single element that triggered Russian revival, it was the leading cause that forced Russia to enhance its role to counter the NATO influence and increase its sphere of influence not only in the region but in the world affairs. The expanding Russian influence is a source of perpetual frustration for the successive US administrations.

Role of Super Powers in the World Politics

Introduction

There are different schools of thoughts in International Relations but Realism is the most prominent and time tested theory of International Relations. At the end of the cold war, realism has emerged as the dominant political thought of the present time. The role of the superpowers in the worlds' politics is very deleterious and they have practically divided the world into different camps and blocs. After the end of the cold war, it was assumed that this phase would be ended but it was just a mere thought. Syria and Ukraine are the new dividing line of superpowers in the present day, where they are overtly and covertly fighting with one another. Arms race and trade wars are shaping the new world orders. China is the emerging economic superpower of the world and the future belongs to Asia and its emerging countries.

What is realism?

Realism can be traced back to thinkers like Machiavelli and Hobbes. Modern proponents include scholars like Hans Joachim Morgenthau (1954), Kenneth Waltz (1979) and John J. Mearsheimer (2001), among many others. The recent versions have rather focused on the structure of the international system and considering it as anarchy. The realism is being followed by the harsh realists like Henry Kissinger, Dr Condoleezza Rice and Presidents of the USA George W Bush and Donald Trump.

Influence of world superpowers in the world politics

According to the encyclopedia Britannica superpower is "Superpower, a state that possesses military or economic might, or both, and general influence vastly superior to that of other states. Scholars generally agree on which state is the foremost or unique superpower, for instance, Britain during the Victorian era and the US after World War II but often disagrees on the criteria that distinguish a superpower from other major powers and, accordingly, on which other states if any should be called superpowers". USA and USSR were the superpowers of the world. After the breakup of the USSR in 1991, only the USA remained the sole superpower of the world. But now Russia is increasing its International power and involving in confrontational politics with the USA. China is the economic superpower of the world and it is increasing its economic might day by day especially in the post-Corona world China has a decisive role.

Ukraine Conflict

The distinctive features of the current international system have done much to shape the pattern of relations between the super-powers and their approaches to third areas. Bipolarity with only two major nuclear powers able to check each other and to pose threats to the entire system imbues relations between the super-powers with an inevitable rivalry. The expanded global system, now encompassing a variety of states and traditions, is culturally more heterogeneous. Because of their varying degrees of control, authority, legitimacy and stability, these new states lack many established dimensions of statehood, making for a less homogeneous system from the point of view of power, and for less cohesion. Ukraine is an example of this perpetual tension between the Russia and USA. Ukrainian rebels are supported by Russia in the greater Russian national interests.

Syrian Conflict

The Muslim world is facing many challenges especially after the fall of the USSR now the world is Unipolar. Syria is an example of it where the existing fault lines of Muslim Ummah was further divided by the world powers. Russians and Americans are fighting in the name of International peace in Syria. It is a clear example of realpolitik.

The distinctive features of the current international system have done much to shape the pattern of relations between the superpowers and their approaches to third areas. In Bipolarity, only two major nuclear powers able to check each other and pose threats to the entire system. On the other hand the relations between the superpowers with an inevitable rivalry. The expanded global system, now encompassing a variety of states and traditions, is culturally more heterogeneous. Because of their varying degrees of control, authority, legitimacy and stability, these new states lack many established dimensions of statehood, making for a less homogeneous system from the point of view of power, and for less cohesion.

Conclusion

The role of the powerful countries in world politics is evident from their distinctive footprints in International affairs. The recent tussles and power politics of international players are there because these players especially superpowers and regional powers are trying to maximize their gains and power and minimizing their losses. The USA is the notorious player in this arena. There must be equilibrium of power or balance of power. And even if their central concepts of 'balance' and 'parity' sound comparable, they should not be mixed up. Only China is the example of a peaceful rise in the world otherwise all the rises of the international powers were based on wars and power politics and the present international politics has no distinction from it.

Russia and Putin

Background

During the cold war, Russia was the arch-rival of the USA. From WWII till 1991 both the superpowers confronted on all the fronts even they tried to dominate space and militarized it. But after the fall of the USSR, they were unable to maintain their Defence budget. Its servicemen were shrunk from 5 million to 1 million and their defence budget from US $ 272 billion to the US $ 14 billion. At the time of dismemberment of the USSR, Putin was Lt Col in KGB who was appointed in East Germany. Later on, he was appointed in President House and also headed FSB. During his security assignments, he was picked by President Boris Yeltsin.

The Phenomenal Rise of Putin

Vladimir Putin had a very humble background. He was born and raised in St. Petersburg. He completed his education in this city and later on joined KGB. He is fluent in English, German and Russian. He is a super tough and highly intelligent person. When he emerged on the surface of Russian politics at that time Russia was facing an economic meltdown, food shortage and corruption. Although he is not free from the charges of corruption he has strongly refuted these allegations. Western media is very critical of his international policies and domestic human rights abuses. He was appointed by Yeltsin in 1999, now for nearly two decades, he is in power. In 2018 he was elected for the fourth time for six years. Western media called him the New Czar of Russia.

President Putin and Russian Revivalism

After the fall of the USSR, there were very limited options in hands with the Russian. 'Survival scenario' was the first option for them. But they were badly failed and already divided into fifteen states. All of their nuclear power remained useless. When Putin came into power he not only stopped the falling economy but also strengthened the Russian international image.

(a) **Syrian Crisis** Russia under Putin had maximum gains in Syria, where they not only outnumbered their rivals i.e. Saudi Arabia, Turkey and the USA. They secured the Bashar regime from falling and brutally destroyed ISIS.

(b) **Iran Ties** Iran is a theocratic state but they have cordial relations with Russia. Many of the Russian scientists are working the Iran nuclear sites and factories. There are around more than one thousand Iranian nuclear sites in Iran. In UN and international forums, Iran is being supported by Putin openly.

(c) **Corona Pandemic** During the corona pandemic Russia was the leading country, who has developed a vaccine. It has strengthened the Russian international image. Sputnik V was a massive achievement of Russia and Putin. Again it has proved that Russia is not a technologically backward country.

(d) **Friendly ties with Turkey** For centuries Turkey and Russia are the arch-rivals. As the successors of the Czars and the Ottoman Kings, this rivalry has centuries of hostilities, but now in an unprecedented move, Russian has handed over the defence systems to the Turks. The USA is astonished by this Russian blow. Putin has won the trust of Turk President Erdogan.

(e) **Partner in Afghanistan** Russia is a partner of the USA and ISAF in Afghanistan. They enjoyed cordial relations with the Northern Alliance of Afghanistan. According to the USA, intelligence reports Putin is supporting the insurgency in Afghanistan. But the USA is unable to stop it.

Conclusion

The revival of Russia is evident in the world, in previous many years Putin has proven his shrewdness in politics at home and abroad. If we can say that he is the most charismatic world leader at this time. He has truly revived Russia militarily, economically and socially. The Russians are blessed that they have Putin which has strengthened not only the Russian international image but it has created a clear cut resistance in front of the American international hegemony.

International Affairs

United Nations and its Collective Security Efforts

Introduction

Humans are considered social animals; they live in societies and fight for their survival. From prehistory to this day humans are striving their best to make themselves secure and prosperous. After WW II the world was divided among two blocs, Soviet Bloc and Western Bloc. The Western bloc under the supervision of the USA started these arrangements and reciprocated by the USSR and its allies. The horizon and objectivity of the UN were sometimes considered biased as they only follow the instructions of permanent five and major power brokers but still UN is the biggest contributor to world peace to date. The UN was founded to be a collective security organization but during the cold war period, the UN was partially unsuccessful to stop international conflicts from happening. UN was successful to stop a direct war between the superpowers. Overtimes the UN role was modified and gradually changed.

UN Military Force

After the failure of the League of Nations, big challenges were lying ahead to the UN. The UN was established to maintain the status quo in the world. Security Council was the prime example of this where the successful powers in WWII were given the lion share in world politics through the UN Security Council. UN worked as a power broker and it was directly involved in the Korean and Congo affair which created a question mark on the credibility of the UN. After WW II the influence of Great Britain and other colonial powers was withering away, the south was demanding more shares in the world economy and resources. Furthermore, it then discusses UN achievements that were not stymied by superpower influence, such as diminishing colonialism, supporting the right to self-determination, serving as a platform for the 'developing world', and endorsing human rights. The charter of the UN rightly acknowledges the right of self-determination and self-defence of all states. UN Charter Article 51 of the Charter, affirming the "inherent right of individual or collective self-defence" of member states, further implied that some conflicts could not be handled within the U.N. framework. This did not happen; however, the emergence of rival power blocs after the war meant that the system for maintaining international peace and security envisaged in the Charter was undermined almost from the outset.

Limited Options for Regional Organizations

These organizations have a limited role to play but these regional organizations in principal are in a better position than the UN to maintain regional peace and stability. UN and her administration give due credit to the regional organizations and the UN charter has legally accepted the role of the regional organizations for the peace and economic prosperity of the world. NATO, SEATO, CENTO, ANZUS and Warsaw Pact like regional security organizations have limited options in hand to secure their vulnerable areas from the hegemony of the other powers.

Cold War and Collective security concept

UN used preventive diplomacy to prevent wars and conflicts. During the cold war, the UN started many collective security efforts to boost world peace but always the meddling of the superpowers of the world distorted the efforts made by the UN. Even the UN was used as a powerful tool against the weaker countries. UN peacekeeping forces were working during the cold war along the Line of Control in Kashmir and on the borders of Arabs and Israel. In Cyprus, they played this role between Turks and Greeks, between Croats and Serbs. They had established zones of sanity during Lebanon civil wars and wars with Israel. Article 43 provides this authority to the UN to call upon force in a time of need. The given table shows all the details of the UN peacekeeping force deployment during the cold war.

Name	Description
U.N. Special Committee on the Balkans (UNSCOB), 1947-51	Investigate guerrilla border crossings into Greece
U.N. Truce Supervisory Organization (UNTSO), 1948-present	Monitor cease-fires along the Israeli border
U.N. Military Observer Group in India and Pakistan (UNMOGIP), 1949-present	Monitor cease-fire in Kashmir
U.N. Emergency Force (UNEF I), 1959-67	Separate Egyptian & Israeli Forces in Sinai.
U.N. Observer Group in Lebanon (UNOGIL), 1958	Monitor infiltration of arms & troops into Lebanon from Syria
U.N. Operation in the Congo (ONUC), 1960-64	Render military assistance, restore civil order
U.N. Temporary Executive Authority (UNTEA), 1962-63	Keep order, administer W. New Guinea in transfer to Indonesia
U.N. Yemen Observer Mission (UNYOM), 1963	Monitor arms infiltration into Yemen.
U.N. Force in Cyprus (UNFICYP), 1964-present	Maintain order, separate Greek/Turk Cypriots.
U.N. India Pakistan Observer Mission (UNIPOM), 1965-66	Monitor cease-fire in 1965
U.N. Emergency Force II (UNEF II), 1974-79	Separate Egyptian & Israeli Forces in Sinai.

U.N. Disengagement Observer Force (UNDOF), 1974-present	Monitor separation of Syrian & Israeli forces on Golan Heights
U.N. Interim Force in Lebanon (UNIFIL), 1978-present	Establish a buffer zone between Israel & Lebanon

Conclusion

UN played a very active role during the cold war conflicts starting from the Korean War till the Afghanistan war. UN played a very decisive role but with every passing day, the role of the UN was decreasing due to the interference of superpowers. Peacekeeping has succeeded primarily where local peoples and political factions have both needed and supported the U.N.'s presence.USA hegemony has changed the world after the fall of communism. U.N. peacekeeping has succeeded in many instances despite considerable organizational, material, and operational shortcomings, in part because troops and commanders on the ground have worked hard to overcome the limitations, sometimes supplying through national channels what was not available through the UN. But UN any operation designed to intervene in situations in which there is only partial local consent is not peacekeeping, but something else and it usually runs into a whole string of problems, as the trials of U.N. forces in Angola, Haiti, Sudan, Bosnia, and Western Sahara currently attest. If the U.N.'s member states continue to send the organization's peacekeepers into politically unstable situations, they risk the political and financial collapse of what has been to date one of the international community's most useful tools for containing and seeking to resolve regional conflicts.

Non-International Armed Conflict

Introduction

Armed conflicts taking place within the territory of a state and in which the armed forces of no other than that own state participate is called a Non-international Armed conflict. There are many examples of this type of armed conflict and in this contemporary world we are facing many problems of these types of conflicts. Another example of this type of armed conflict is that in which armed violence between state and those regarded as dissidents, terrorist or insurgents groups. There may be one or more than one group involves in conflict and may or may not be the state forces involve in it.

What is Non-International Armed Conflict?

Non-international armed conflicts are protracted armed confrontations occurring between governmental armed forces and the forces of one or more armed groups or between such groups arising on the territory of a State, the armed confrontation must reach a minimum level of intensity and the parties involved in the conflict must show a minimum of organization.

It is on this basis that the ICR takes this opportunity to present the prevailing legal opinion on the definition of *"international armed conflict"* and *"non-international armed conflict"* under International Humanitarian Law, the branch of international law which governs armed conflict. International humanitarian law distinguishes two types of armed conflicts, namely:

> ➤ **International armed conflict** International armed conflicts, opposing two or more States.
> ➤ **Non-international armed conflict** between, governmental forces and non-governmental armed groups or between such groups only. International Humanitarian Law (IHL) treaty law also establishes a distinction between non-international armed conflicts in the meaning of common Article 3 of the Geneva Conventions of 1949 and non-international armed conflicts falling within the definition provided in Art. 1 of Additional Protocol II.

Protocol II defines a non-international armed conflict for the purposes of the Protocol as one "which takes place in the territory of a Party to the Protocol between its armed forces and dissident armed forces or other organized armed groups". It then stipulates that the dissident forces must be "under responsible command, exercise such control over a part of its territory as to enable them to carry out sustained and concerted military operations and to implement this Protocol". Protocol II states quite clearly that it "shall not apply to situations of internal disturbances and tensions, such as riots, isolated and sporadic acts of violence and other acts of a similar nature," as these are not considered to be armed conflicts. So generally this is a conflict in which state forces participate against armed rebels, insurgents etc.

Non-International Armed Conflict Examples

In the world we have many examples of Non-International Arms conflicts starting from our own region Baluchistan insurgency, TTP, Kashmir freedom movement, Rohigya issue, Syrian issue, Libyan problem, Kurds struggle etc are few examples of these armed conflicts although there is a diversity of the issues, ideologies and background. Recently the Non International Conflicts have come closer to the International conflicts like the Bosnian issue which came under the International Criminal Court and Rwanda issue was also taken up by the court. This study comes to the conclusion that 136 (and arguably even 141) out of 161 rules of customary humanitarian law, many of which run parallel to rules of Protocol I applicable as a treaty to international armed conflicts, apply equally to non-international armed conflicts.

International Humanitarian Law (IHL)

All these conflicts came under the jurisdiction of IHL. Article 3 common to all four Geneva Conventions represents the first attempt to lay down rules governing non-international armed conflicts. It has been described as a "convention in miniature" because it contains within it the basic minimum standards of international humanitarian law applicable in conflict situations. The International Court of Justice reinforced this view, stating that the rules in common Article 3 reflect elementary considerations of humanity applicable under customary international law to any armed conflict.

Fundamental guarantees

All persons not directly participating in the conflict or who have ceased to do so because, for example, they are hors de combat or have surrendered are entitled to be treated humanely and to receive respect for their person, religious practices, honour and convictions without adverse distinction. Under Protocol II it is prohibited to order that there will be no survivors In addition, Protocol II contains a catalogue of fundamental guarantees prohibiting at anytime and anywhere:

- ➢ Violence to life, health and physical or mental wellbeing of persons, in particular murder as well as cruel treatment such as torture, mutilation or any form of corporal punishment
- ➢ Collective punishments
- ➢ Taking of hostages
- ➢ Acts of terrorism
- ➢ Outrages upon personal dignity, in particular humiliating and degrading treatment, rape, enforced prostitution and any form of indecent assault
- ➢ Slavery and the slave trade in all their forms
- ➢ Pillage
- ➢ Threats to commit any of the foregoing acts

Protection of children

Children under 15 years are exempted to take part in armed conflicts

Protection of women

Women are made protected from forced labour and sex

Treatment of detainees

Detainees and POWs are to be treated as per IHL

Trial and punishment guaranteed

Fair trial has been guaranteed

Amnesty encouraged

General amnesty has been encouraged

Wounded and sick care

Human life is very vital to protect so medical treatment is guaranteed to all

Civilian population

All types of civil population are protected from mass bombing etc.

Conclusion

So Non-international armed conflicts, is a conflict between governmental forces and non-governmental armed groups, or between such groups only. IHL treaty law also establishes a distinction between non-international armed conflicts in the meaning of common. There are many Non international Conflicts taking place in the world but International Humanitarian Law (IHL) is unable to protect the people because the powerful countries of the world have drawn different lines for them. Itself IHL is very smart work but its limited utilization has challenged the world's peace.

Multinational Companies (MNCs) and their Global Impacts

Introduction

Globalization is a new term and it is the result of advancement in transportation. Information Technology (IT), Communication and business. It explains the ever-growing economic micro-socio, political technological and cultural linkages that link individual, communities, businesses and government around the globe. Globalization also involves the growth of multinational corporations MNCs and transnational corporations TNCs.

Due to the recent development in communication and presence of Mass Media this world is becoming a global village and nations are now that much closely netted that their interdependence has much increased. Their nationalistic behaviour has also been changed and supranational feelings are emerging. In this era of modernism, international business has changed into a global form and Multinational/transnational Companies have taken over the world economies and they have surpassed the national economies also.

Due to the recent development in communication and presence of Mass Media this world is becoming a global village and nations are now that much closely netted that their interdependence has much increased. Their nationalistic behaviour has also been changed and supranational feelings are emerging. In this era of modernism, international business has changed into a global form and Multinational/transnational Companies have taken over the world economies and they have surpassed the national economies also. These companies are called Multinational Corporation (MNCs). These MNCs are controlling the policies of the governments, especially economic and foreign policies are being controlled by them.

Multinational Corporation (MNC)

According to Holm and Sorenson, a definition of globalization is "the intensification of economic, political, social and cultural relations across borders. A multinational corporation (MNC) has facilities and other assets in at least one country other than the home country. These companies have offices, workforce and factories in different countries and usually have a centralized head office where they coordinate global management. Very large multinationals have budgets that exceed those of many small countries. So MNCs are those companies that are operating internationally with a bulk of the investment. They are considered more powerful than the countries. They are that much powerful that they can easily influence the policies of the countries.

What is Globalization?

Globalization is a new term and it is the result of advancement in transportation. Information Technology (IT), Communication and business. It explains the ever-growing socio-economic, political technological and cultural linkages that link individual, communities, businesses and government around the globe. Globalization also involves the growth of multinational corporations (MNCs) and transnational corporations (TNCs). According to the Peterson Institute of International Economics, 'Globalization' is the word used to describe the growing interdependence of the world's economies, cultures, and populations, brought about by cross-border trade in goods and services, technology, and flows of investment, people, and information.

Host societies and Challenges imposed by MNCs

There are two-dimensional impacts of MNCs on host societies one is positive and the other is a negative impact. The positive effects are these

Good business practices Good governance, transparency within the organization, delegation of power, performance-based evaluation and incentives program encourages the merit-based approach. The work culture and the professional working environment within the organization are important

Comforts of life The economies of scale, quality control and healthy competition in certain cases lead to price cuts and other incentives to the end-user. People get the comforts of life at much cheaper rates and /or at their doorsteps.

Improvement of Infrastructure Many MNCs help in improving the infrastructure and provision of basic needs in their specific areas of operation. They do it directly or provide funds to civil society organizations or give direct charity to improve the living and business conditions in areas where they are operating. While in many cases these are voluntary practices, the tax exemption facility provided under the law also helps in encouraging such initiatives. Because of MNCs, a kind of interaction across the boundaries takes place. Even education has to take into account the global perspectives

Characteristics of MNCs As MNCs are trendsetters, these practices are also followed by large national corporations. Even civil society is influenced by this professional culture. The merit and knowledge-based professional culture lead to the promotion of more efficient management and better business education along with other important disciplines in society.

Financial and technical resources and expertise There is no denying the fact that the MNCs bring in certain advantages to the host societies. Huge resources and investments, technology, innovation and expertise are made available to host societies through these MNCs. A culture of research and development, training in marketing and developing human resource within the organization is also beneficial for the host societies. MNCs also contribute significantly to the exchequer by paying taxes

Global Perspectives education and cross-cultural understanding increase the adaptability of the students anywhere in the world. This leads to the mixing of cultures and practices and encourages pluralism as well as competition. Out-sourcing by MNCs particularly in services sectors is relatively a new but important phenomenon. The host countries are thus becoming not just the workshop of the world but the back office too. Besides providing employment this is also promoting pluralism. These can be great assets for society if addressed positively.

Drawbacks of MNCs

Increasing materialism and consumption The type of development, being promoted is based on mere material gains. Luxuries and comforts are being turned into needs and necessities. Thus happiness and satisfaction are being associated with luxuries and their acquisition. Thanks to MNCs, "the consumption culture" has overtaken almost the whole world, though it first took hold of the developed world.

Excessive expansion of credit The new credit culture is changing the attitudes towards loans. Loans are being encouraged to facilitate the acquisition of the luxuries of life. The offer of easy credit, consumer financing, credit cards and personal loans by the banks to the middle class is promoting a culture of living beyond means. Lifestyles are changing because of it, and not necessarily for the better.

Corruption and crime Greediness, disparities and a sense of deprivation, along with the race to acquire new products are also giving rise to corruption and crime. The focus is on acquiring money in whichever manner it comes; even through illegal means if it is not available through legitimate sources. On their part, MNCs also corrupt people to capture markets.

The brain drains The term 'brain drain' is usually used for talent going towards other countries in search of higher income. MNCs have involved in yet another kind of brain drain. With their capacity to pay, they can hire the most qualified and experienced talent available in society. Those working with MNCs consider themselves as part of an elite class associated with the global community. Consequently, most of them develop a culture that makes them less relevant to their societies.

Family Fabric The culture and lifestyle changes coming in with the spread of MNCs' influence in society are proving lethal for the family fabric of host societies. Overspending and living beyond means are creating economic pressures, tensions and stress within families. Various indicators prove that women working with the MNCs and other big organizations are under stress when entering into marriages and bearing children. Parents have little time for their family, particularly children.

Conclusion

MNCs are affecting both individual and state and their impact is very deep and it is eroding the old cultural values but the investment made by the MNCs is very lucrative and it can change the destiny of the small economies. It is upon those countries to devise a mechanism to protect themselves from the negative impacts of globalization and maximize their benefits from the global investment made by the MNCs

Sources of International law

Introduction

The character of modern international law, and its transformations, depends upon the structure of the modern state system and the changing political groupings which have developed within that system. Permanent diplomacy is a characteristic of the modern state system. Hand in Hand the theory and practice of the balance of power gradually advances. In the Middle Ages, emperors and popes, princes, etc. maintained relations with their opponents, concluded treaties with them and treated them as legitimate adversaries in armed conflict. The idea of maintaining a minimum standard of international legal relations with the opponents based on natural law, which was generally recognized as binding for all peoples, corresponded broadly to the practical needs of commercial intercourse in the world.

What is International Law?

International law is the name of a body of rules which regulate the conduct of the States in their relations with one another. Sources of international law include treaties, international customs, general principles of law as recognized by civilized nations, the decisions of national and lower courts, and scholarly writings. International Law is considered as a weaker law when we have its comparison with the local laws of the sovereign states. International Law has the materials and processes out of which the rules and principles regulating the international community are developed. They have been influenced by a range of political and legal theories.

Sources of International Law

There are different sources of International Law. We extract from the sources and these sources have different legal grandness and importance.

(a)   Treaties and conventions Different treaties and conventions signed by the state can become part of International Law

(b)   International Custom Just like the British Constitution major part of it is based on customs same like that many International customs can be transformed as International Law.

(c)   General Principles of Municipal Law Some general rules and principals of the municipal laws become the part of International Law

(d)   Subsidiary Sources of judicial decisions and legal publications Although it is not binding many decisions made by the Federal courts or Supreme Courts are taking as the internationally implementable law rulings.

Area covered by International Law

Statute of the International Court of Justice (ICJ) Article 38 shows what are the areas covered by International Law.

(1)   The Court, whose function is to decide by International Law such disputes as are submitted to it, shall apply

(2)   International Conventions, whether general or particular establishing rules expressly recognized by the contesting states

(3)   International Custom, as evidence of general practice, accepted as law

(4)   The general principles of law recognized by civilized nations

(5)   Subject to the provisions of Article 59, judicial decisions and the teachings of the most highly qualified publicists of the various nations, as a subsidiary, means for the determination of rules of law

Other sources of law

> Unilateral acts of State, such as recognition
> Resolutions of International Organizations

Are These Accurate Reflections Of The Sources Of International Law?

The sources are not completely accurate, treaties are responsible for the formation of important Intergovernmental organizations like the UN and EU, the organization are cardinal to national and 'International concerns'. Treaties produced the constitutions of these organizations and birthed them especially the UN that has powerful organs like the Security Council and General Assembly that control the affairs of the world by Resolutions. Treaties and Resolutions by General Assembly are 'law making' means. The positivist scholar believes that treaties and international custom now tend towards legal positivism; they share the opinion that international law is binding only if it is rooted in state consent and that no other sources exist except consent found in treaty and custom.

Treaty was criticized because its processes are 'political', that is 'involving law-making primarily by diplomatic means rather than codification and progressive development by legal experts' and weaknesses in custom for its lack of visibility and slow formation process. Furthermore, one cannot say that the source is perfect in as much as positivist finds expression in the 'sources' particularly treaty and custom which their formulation process could be slow and the inability of these to change with the speed of international law and the solution is to keep the law out of strict positivism to adapt to a new system of 'legislation and administrative rule making' The states belong to UN and UN does produce vast amounts of law, that is law made by the system. The legislative ability of the UN has escalated from a 'horizontal' system based upon state consent towards a more 'hierarchical' system, it is submitted that the accuracy of international law can at least be found in this if not found.

Conclusion

All the sources discussed above can all be found in the practice of the UN and where they cannot be found they kowtow and bow to the resolutions of the Security Council and it will remain binding on members and even on non-members, aberration of which can be faced with sanctions. It is submitted that the UN has provided a true compliment for the gap created in what is supposed to be an accurate reflection of other sources of international law and its activities have positively affected lawmaking ways by resolutions and faster means by 15 members of Security Council and 193 members of the General Assembly as greater needs arise for fast development of international law codified by International law commission.

Non-international conflicts and International Law

Introduction

Human are social animals but these social animals are always struggling to survive and the question of survival is the real struggle of existence. Humans are at war with one another for their survival and they fought a war for control of the resources. Armed conflicts take place within the territory of a state and in which the armed forces of no other than that own state participate is called a Non-international Armed conflict. There are many examples of this type of armed conflict and in this contemporary world; we are facing many problems of these types of conflicts. Another example of this type of armed conflict is that in which armed violence between the state and those regarded as dissidents, rebel or insurgents groups. There may be one or more than one group involves in conflict and may or may not be the state forces involve in it. So non-international arms conflicts are taking place in different parts of the world and generally, they are not directly linked with external involvement.

Non-International Armed Conflict and Humanitarian Law

What is a non-international arms conflict? Non-international armed conflicts are protracted armed confrontations occurring between governmental armed forces and the forces of one or more armed groups or between such groups arising on the territory of a State. It means state versus non-state insurgent, revolutionary rebel or terrorist group. The armed confrontation must reach a minimum level of intensity and the parties involved in the conflict must show a minimum of organization. International Humanitarian Law (ILW) deals with the protection of humans during the crisis, especially during conflicts and wars. During the war, the soldiers are killed and the civilian population also comes under attack. During WWI and WWII millions of people were killed during these wars. To protect the prisoners of wars from prosecutions and atrocities third Geneva Convention of POWs was passed and till it has been ratified by the 196 states. It is on this basis that the ICR takes this opportunity to present the prevailing legal opinion on the definition of "international armed conflict" and "non-international armed conflict" under International Humanitarian Law, the branch of international law which governs armed conflict. International humanitarian law distinguishes two types of armed conflicts, namely:

(a)   International armed conflicts, opposing two or more States.

(b)   Non-international armed conflicts, between governmental forces and non-governmental armed groups, or between such groups only. IHL treaty law also establishes a distinction between non-international armed conflicts in the meaning of common Article 3 of the Geneva Conventions of 1949 and non-international armed conflicts falling within the definition provided in Article 1 of Additional Protocol II.

Protocol II defines a non-international armed conflict for the Protocol as one "which takes place in the territory of a Party to the Protocol between its armed forces and dissident armed forces or other organized armed groups". It then stipulates that the dissident forces must be "under responsible command, exercise such control over a part of its territory as to enable them to carry out sustained and concerted military operations and to implement this Protocol". Protocol II states quite clearly that it "shall not apply to situations of internal disturbances and tensions, such as riots, isolated and sporadic acts of violence and other acts of a similar nature," as these are not considered to be armed conflicts. Generally, these conflicts deal with the insurgency inside a country and low-level violence triggered by the violent groups for pressurizing their demands.

Relevance of law in non-international conflicts

All these conflicts came under the jurisdiction of IHL. Article 3 common to all four Geneva Conventions represent the first attempt to lay down rules governing non-international armed conflicts. It has been described as a "convention in miniature" because it contains within it the basic minimum standards of international humanitarian law applicable in conflict situations. The International Court of Justice reinforced this view, stating that the rules in common Article 3 reflect elementary considerations of humanity applicable under customary international law to any armed conflict.

(a)   Fundamental guarantees

All persons not directly participating in the conflict or who have ceased to do so because, for example, they are hors de combat or have surrendered are entitled to be treated humanely and to receive respect for their person, religious practices, honour and convictions without adverse distinction. Under Protocol II it is prohibited to order that there will be no survivors Besides, Protocol II contains a catalogue of fundamental guarantees prohibiting at any time and anywhere:

- Violence to life, health and physical or mental wellbeing of persons, in particular, murder as well as cruel treatment such as torture, mutilation or any form of corporal punishment
- Collective punishments
- Taking of hostages
- Acts of terrorism
- Outrages upon personal dignity, in particular humiliating and degrading treatment, rape, enforced prostitution and any form of indecent assault
- Slavery and the slave trade in all their forms

> Threats to commit any of the foregoing acts

(b)   Protection of children/ women

Children less than 15 years are exempted to take part in armed conflicts that why the UN can impose restrictions on any country that is involved in these heinous crimes. Women are the most vulnerable part of the war and they are made sex slaves and brutally tortured and made sex slaves. Women are made protected from forced labour and sex.

(c)   Civilian population/car of wounded and sick

Human life is very vital to protect so medical treatment is guaranteed to all. All types of the civil population are protected from mass bombing/ carpet bombing and genocide.

(d)   Treatment of detainees

Detainees and POWs are to be treated as per IHL and they are not prosecuted without fair trial and there must be fairness in all the court proceedings against them.

Conclusion

There are many Non-international Conflicts taking place in the world but International Humanitarian Law is unable to protect the people because the powerful countries of the world have drawn different lines for them. IHL is very smart work but the implementation of the law is very week. Non-international armed conflicts are a conflict between government forces and non-governmental armed groups or between such groups only. International Humanitarian Law treaty (IHL) law also establishes a distinction between non-international armed conflicts. UN has been failed to implement this law in non-international armed conflicts especially in Asian and African countries where repressive regimes continuously suppress the genuine movement for change.

Brinkmanship

What is Brinkmanship?

According to the encyclopedia, Britannica Brinkmanship is a "foreign policy practice in which one or both parties force the interaction between them to the threshold of confrontation to gain an advantageous negotiation position over the other. The technique is characterized by aggressive risk-taking policy choices that court potential disaster" and according to the Marriam Webster dictionary meaning is "the art or practice of pushing a dangerous situation or confrontation to the limit of safety especially to force the desired outcome"

Although the practice of brinkmanship has probably existed since the dawn of human history, the origin of the word comes from a 1956 Life magazine interview with former U.S. secretary of state John Foster Dulles, in which he claimed that, in diplomacy, "if you are scared to go to the brink (of war), you are lost." In response, American politician and diplomat Adlai Stevenson derided Dulles's "brinksmanship" as reckless. It is a risky game where the politicians take the maximum risks for the maximum gains through going at the edge of war or utilizing the maximum of the pressure.

Use of brinkmanship

The term was used repeatedly during the Cold War, a period characterized by tense relations between the United States and the Soviet Union. It marked a significant change in the conduct of foreign policy. Whereas the interaction between states had previously been predicated on the balance of power (BOP) largely based on a state's economic and military power and the desire to prevent any major shifts in the status quo a state's possession of nuclear weapons created an entirely new set of foreign policy tools, which it could use to influence others.

Perhaps the best-documented case of brinkmanship was the Soviet placement of nuclear missiles in Cuba in 1962 and the U.S. response, which is now referred to as the Cuban missile crisis. Soviet Premier Nikita Khrushchev sought to defend Cuba from the U.S. and to extend Soviet strategic power in the region by secretly placing medium and intermediate-range ballistic missiles (IBMs) in Cuba, which threatened much of the continental United States. Instead of gaining a leveraged position over the U.S., Khrushchev's brinkmanship almost brought the U.S. and Soviet Union to nuclear war. The crisis concluded after U.S. President John F. Kennedy revealed the presence of Khrushchev's weapons and ordered a naval "quarantine" around Cuba, which resulted in the Soviet Union withdrawing its missiles.

International Relations and Abstract Concepts of Morality and Ethics

Introduction

There are different schools of thoughts in International Relations which represent different concepts and ideas. Realism is the oldest school of thought and the majority of the scholars follow this school of thought but here we are going to discuss the concept of 'Idealism' in IR. Idealism is the opposite of realism. Idealism has emerged as the most positive, optimistic and productive school of thought in IR. Realism has destroyed the world by engaging countries in wars, proxies and 'zero-sum games' but on the other hand, Idealism has shown the new vistas of cooperation and universal values of collaboration, morality, ethics and humanism assistance are propagated through it.

Why there is a need for morality, ethics and Law in IR?

At the end of the cold war, realism has emerged as the dominant political thought of the present time. The role of the superpowers in the worlds' politics was very deleterious and they have practically divided the world into different camps and blocs.

After the end of the cold war, it was assumed that this phase has been ended but it was just a mere contemplation. Syria and Ukraine are the new dividing line of superpowers in the present day, where they are overtly and covertly fighting with one another. China is the emerging economic superpower of the world. Afghanistan, Vietnam, Libya, Yemen and Iraq are the example of realist politics. But on the other hand, United Nations, European Union, ICJ, and Geneva Conventions are the example of the moral and ethical thinking of cooperation. Without law, this world would be a jungle and in the Jungle who rules, who has the power to protect itself and punish its opponents. So morality, ethics and laws are necessary for the smooth functioning of the world.

Idealism and Contemporary World

In general parlance on international matters, idealism is a term applied to any idea, goal, or practise considered to be impractical. Thus eradicating nuclear weapons is considered idealistic, as is substituting open for secret diplomacy, entrusting international security to the UN, creating an African Union on the model of the EU, or the global eradication of poverty and injustice. The bases of such judgments are rarely made explicit, but they usually rest on a pessimistic reading of human nature along with a historical judgment on the difficulty of peaceably achieving radical change in world affairs.

The distinctive features of the current international system have done much to shape the pattern of relations between the superpowers and the rest of the world. Idealism is the approach that has open new doors for cooperation among the world states and this approach has made them think out of the box by extending their hands for cooperation by setting aside the realpolitik.

Examples from Contemporary world order

This present-day world and modern-day society is nothing without cooperation and rule of law. This world is full of examples of cooperation based on morality ethics and law. Here are those examples

(a)   Regional cooperation

There are different regional organizations for regional cooperation in the contemporary world. These regional organizations are inspired by the E.U model. ASEAN, NAFTA, African Union are examples of these organizations which has transformed this world from competition to cooperation. Due to this global trade has increased many folds.

(b)   Eradication of the Social evils

Poverty, terrorism, food security, natural calamities, diseases and unequal growth are few problems out of the sea of different problems. The social evils are other problem can be eradicated with the help of true implementation of the International Law.

(c)   Millennium development goals

The millennium development goals were set by the UN for this millennium. The United Nations Millennium Declaration, signed in September 2000 commits world leaders to combat poverty, hunger, disease, illiteracy, environmental degradation, and discrimination against women. The MDGs are derived from this Declaration, and all have specific targets and indicators. The Eight Millennium Development Goals are:

- ➢ To eradicate extreme poverty and hunger
- ➢ To achieve universal primary education
- ➢ To promote gender equality and empower women
- ➢ To reduce child mortality
- ➢ To improve maternal health
- ➢ To combat HIV/aids, malaria, and other diseases
- ➢ To ensure environmental sustainability
- ➢ To develop a global partnership for the development

These goals are idealistically set and to fulfil these goals there is a requirement of international cooperation. If these goals are achieved then this world would be a different place to live in.

(d) Atomic for peace

International Morality consists of moral principles which are endorsed by several nations. The rules of customary International Law reflect International morality. One of the major sources and sanctions of International Law has been International Morality. Atomic bombs were made for human destruction but now dozens of States are cooperating in the field of atomic for peace. These states are running nuclear plants for the generation of electricity; atomic is used for disease control and scientific development in the field of food technology. So we can easily judge that international relations are in dire need of following the moral, ethical and law-based principles to make this world a better prosperous and safer world.

Conclusion

Idealism stands for improving and improvising international relations by eliminating international evil through cooperation and multilateral engagements at a supra-national level. To remove these evils strong human will is required which can eradicate the evils and extend cooperation. In conclusion, idealism can be said to be a functional approach to studying international relations because it explains several trends that are occurring in the current international order. The League of Nations showed how the idealist view of human nature as rational and good became the foundation of the UN and the international community. The idealist belief of man as rational underpins the idea that through morality law and ethics all the problems can be solved. It also explains why free trade capitalism is the dominant economic global policy not only in Europe but also in Africa and Asia. The abstract concepts of ethics morality are not vague but the future of human existence is based on these concepts and these will change the density of man soon.

Middle East

Muslim World and Pakistan

Introduction

It was a "Facebook Revolution" or "Arab spring" which jolted the Muslim world from Tunis to Bahrain and created ripple effects and small seismic waves for Saudia, Yemen, and Qatar. The deep impacts of these waves were seen in Syria Libya and Egypt, where the strong waves of change have uprooted and shacked the old system only Syria was able to sustain it but at the cost of thousands of deaths.

The Arab Spring

The Arab Spring was a significant set of changes, involving an unparalleled mobilization of people in many parts of the Arab world. In Egypt, it led to the downfall of the regime of Hosni Mubarak, who had ruled the country as a de facto dictator for 30 years. The broad-based mobilization unleashed by these events continued after Mubarak's fall, underscoring the importance of the power of the street. Several theories in social science emphasize the role of De facto power, often resulting from groups being able to solve their collective action problems and mobilizing in the street, in changing economic allocations, and even in changing the de jure distribution of political power. Nevertheless, there is only limited evidence in economics and other social sciences showing that changes in the de facto political power of different groups and political mobilization directly matter for any economic outcome.

Turmoil in the Middle East and Pakistan

Winds of change are blowing in the Arab West Asia and North Africa. Many commentators have been speculating that the unrest would remain confined to the region. Whether Pakistan would be spared from this kind of large scale popular revolt is an issue that calls for a separate examination, given its fragile social and political system and an almost stagnant economy. The relevant question now is that as the new Middle East evolves how this will affect the country's relations with the region.

In recent years, Pakistan has been drifting away from its South Asian roots towards the Arab Middle East, especially Saudi Arabia and the Gulf States. The current situation in the Middle East should persuade the people at the helm of affairs to rethink this false endeavour. Whatever pattern the current revolution will take, it is reasonable to argue that with time, the Middle East will never be the same again. In the meantime, they will try to defend the status quo in Bahrain, where their troops are now stationed to support the Sunni al-Khalifa family ruling over the Shia majority. If the Shias should win there, this would have repercussions concerning their Shia population, and will also boost Iran's position. Similarly, in Yemen, the president who has ruled the country for 32 years with an iron grip was getting support to resist change but brutally killed.

There are two notable regional players, Iran and Saudi Arabia, who have a direct stake in the changes which are taking place in the Middle East. And in the international arena, what role the US as well as China plan to pursue will have an important impact on the situation. All four of them have overlapping and conflicting objectives. The Middle East has always been an arena for this kind of diplomatic game.

The current situation in the Middle East should persuade the people at the helm of affairs to rethink this false endeavour. Whatever pattern the current revolution will take, it is reasonable to argue that over time, the Middle East will never be the same again. To stem this tide the Saudi monarchy, for example, is beginning to sense the danger, but does not realize that offering stipends and subsidies will not meet the basic needs of the younger generation. Nor will the tokenism introduce municipal self-government. Then, there are questions about human rights, not only for the Shia minority but for women as well. The country needs social and economic reconstruction.

Egypt, not Saudi Arabia, holds a unique position in the Middle East and is destined to play an important role in the outcome in the region. How the revolution will play out in that country is difficult to answer. The movement can be in danger of getting compromised if elections are either too early or too late. And then the part the Muslim Brotherhood would play would have a significant effect on the political structure which will replace the system developed by Hosni Mubarak. At present, the party is engaged in a vigorous internal debate about democracy and its place in the new political system in the country. It is important to note as well that with Mubarak removed from the scene, there will be no status quo ante for Israel.

Current Situation

Looking at the rest of the Middle East, Algeria has an authoritarian regime and at present is living through a post-civil war trauma, which was bloody and cost around 200,000 casualties. Recently the government lifted the state of emergency. Morocco seems to have escaped this windstorm, with an accommodating monarchy and a stable political system. Jordan is trying to contain its unrest. The current main trouble spots are Libya and Syria. There are two notable regional players, Iran and Saudi Arabia, who have a direct stake in the changes which are taking place in the Middle East. And in the international arena, what role the US as well as China plan to pursue will have an important impact on the situation. All four of them have overlapping and conflicting objectives. The Middle East has always been an arena for this kind of diplomatic game.

Role of Foreign Powers

The US, for example, supports stability in Yemen and Bahrain from the point of view of its security. In Libya, however, it agreed to start the no-fly zone provided there was regional support for it. This was offered by the Arab League, where Saudi Arabia is an important member. In NATO, Turkey is a reluctant ally and supports an early ceasefire. If this should come to pass, then Libya would become a divided country, with rebels holding on to the areas on which they have gained effective control. How would China view this development will depend on how it can save its interest in Libyan oil, though it must be worried about the tottering of Middle East dominoes, representing authoritarian doctrines.

Syria has been under a secular, single-party Ba'athist rule with Bashar al-Assad as president. His father, Hafez al-Assad established the regime with the liberalized but state-dominated economy, broadly on the Chinese model. The Ba'athist party has a strong grip on Syrian politics. Hafez al-Assad, for example, is known for having ruthlessly suppressed a revolt by Muslim Brotherhood when he bombed the city of Hama to kill about 35,000 people in 1982. Turkey's Tayyib Erdogan has advised Bashar al-Assad to implement the reforms without delay.

Relatives of the Assad family pervade the government and dominate the economy. The Ba'athist party has a strong grip on Syrian politics. Hafez al-Assad, for example, is known for having ruthlessly suppressed a revolt by Muslim Brotherhood when he bombed the city of Hama to kill about 35,000 people in 1982. Bashar inherited the notorious emergency laws from his father's regime after his father's death in 2000. The civilian campaign is focused on these emergency laws. Turkey's Recep Tayyib Erdogan has advised Bashar al-Assad to implement the reforms without delay. but like all the tyrants he is unwilling to implement the reforms. Saudia and Iran are playing tug of war in the Muslim world and the outcomes are very hilarious for the Muslims. In this situation, only a few Muslim countries are neutral like Pakistan, Malaysia and Turkey. These countries can play a game-changer role and can stop the Domino effect of 'Arab spring' which has devastated the Muslim world. Western powers are playing the role of power brokers and disturbed the map of the Muslim world. Now Pakistan must maintain the status quo and try to end hostilities between Iran and Saudia.

Conclusion

The Muslim world a vast construct of over 1.5 billion souls stretching from Southeast Asia to the Sahara is today facing a unique series of tumultuous events. Extremist militants have unleashed an orgy of violence across vast swaths of the Middle East, Asia and Africa Stakes are high concerning the stability of Syria for Iran, a `strategic ally of the country. It is through Syrian conduit that the Shia groups in Beirut get support from Iran, and Hamas is also a direct beneficiary of this arrangement. One could safely assume that Saudi Arabia is not going to escape the winds of change blowing across the entire Arab World. It would be in the interests of Pakistan, as a South Asian nation, to maintain the status quo in the region and partially support the emerging progressive forces in the Middle East, and not endorse the reactionary status quo seekers loaded with petro-dollar diplomacy. The longer interests of the 'Ummah' must be considered in mind. Turkey and Pakistan are the countries with a strong military and middle class which can pacify the upheaval and foreign interference in the Muslim world. Turkey and Pakistan can the model democracies for the Muslim world if and only if they can transform them and adapt to changes. Pakistan is a key player, who influences Saudia and Iran.

Yemen Conflict

Introduction

The present-day Muslim world is facing many problems. The problems are directly related to the post /11 shocks being faced by the Muslim world especially by the Arab World. The Arab world has been completely devastated by the shock waves inflicted by the 'Arab Spring'. Tunisia, Egypt, Libya, Syria and Yemen were the most affected by these pseudo revolutions. The Arab Spring was a significant set of changes, involving an unparalleled mobilization of people in many parts of the Arab world. The broad-based mobilization unleashed by these events continued after Mubarak's fall, underscoring the importance of the power of the street. The political unrest, youth bulge and limited say of the people in the political system has made people, politically so aware. They were highly unsatisfied by their governments and political systems which had limited or no delivery system.

Whatever pattern the current revolution will take, it is reasonable to argue that over time, the Middle East will never be the same again. In the meantime, they will try to defend the status quo in Bahrain, where their troops are now stationed to support the

Sunni al-Khalifa family ruling over the Shia majority. If the Shias should win there, this would have repercussions regarding their Shia population, and will also boost Iran's position. Similarly, in Yemen, the president who has ruled the country for 32 years with an iron grip was getting support to resist change but brutally killed.

Background of the Conflict

There are two notable regional players, Iran and Saudi Arabia, who have a direct stake in the changes which are taking place in the Middle East. And in the international arena, what role the US as well as China plan to pursue will have an important impact on the situation. All four of them have overlapping and conflicting objectives. The Middle East has always been an arena for this kind of diplomatic game. The Arab spring has changed the political landscape of the Middle East

The Yemen conflict and Present situation

The current situation in the Middle East should persuade the people at the helm of affairs, to rethink this false endeavour. Whatever pattern the current revolution will take, it is reasonable to argue that with time, the Middle East will never be the same again. To stem this tide the Saudi monarchy, for example, is beginning to sense the danger, but does not realize that offering stipends and subsidies will not meet the basic needs of the younger generation. No one will be satisfied by the limited or controlled democracy. Then, there are questions about human rights, not only for the Shia minority but for women as well. The country needs social and economic reconstruction.

In November 2014 President Saleh agrees to hand over power to his deputy, Abdrabbuh Mansour Hadi, after months of protests. A united government including the prime minister from the opposition formed. Hadi was failed to stop Al Qaeda attacks. In 2014 Houthi rebels occupied the major parts of the capital Sana. In 2015 civil war was broke out between Hadi and Shia Houthi rebels and Al Qaeda became a party also till now this war is on.

Yemen currently has the greatest level of humanitarian needs in the world. According to a report, nearly 16 million are in emergency needs. Nearly 10000 people are killed and two million are displaced, looking for shelter from disease and violence. The war in Yemen is having a disproportionate impact on Yemeni women and girls, who are exposed to increased risk of violence, exploitation and abuse while having a harder time accessing basic health care, including maternal and child health. 1.8 million Children are suffering from acute malnutrition, of which 400,000 children under five are suffering from severe acute malnutrition. There are about 1.1 million malnourished pregnant and breastfeeding females. More than 3.25 million womenfolk in Yemen are facing bigger health and protection risks. Starvation and famine are a straight result of conflict and can only fully be eradicated by bringing the battle to an end

According to the UNHCR, there are 22.2 million Yemenis now in need of humanitarian assistance. Those forced to flee their homes are especially at risk. Nearly 2 million people now languish in desperate conditions, away from home and deprived of basic needs.

Conclusion

The Muslim world a vast construct of over 1.5 billion souls stretching from Southeast Asia to the Sahara is today facing a unique series of tumultuous events. Extremist militants have unleashed an orgy of violence across vast swaths of the Middle East, Asia and Africa Stakes are high concerning the stability of Yemen a strategic ally of Saudi Arabia. It is Iran which is supporting Shia groups in Yemen and Saudia was supporting the Mansoor Hadi government. This problem is not destabilizing the Arab Peninsula but it is a destructive event for the unity of the Muslim Ummah.

Role of Propaganda in Iraq War

Introduction

The Iraq war is taken as a major media event in the world and in both the wars of 1992 and 2003; media became frenzy to cover the event. The leading newspapers and TV channels covered the event in different spectrums. The major take away from their viewpoint was that Iraq is a tyrant state and Saddam Hussian is a bloodthirsty monster, who is highly ambitious and greedy. The main cause of the attack was the reports about "weapon of mass destruction" (WMD). President Bush Junior was preparing for the war on Iraq after 9/11 but he has to wait for two years. The UN mandated against the destruction of weapons of mass destruction (WMD). But the USA attacked unilaterally on Iraq in 2003.

What is propaganda?

According to the Encyclopedia Britannica propaganda is, "dissemination of information facts, arguments, rumours, half-truths, or lies to influence public opinion". The other concept about the propaganda is a theory of Propaganda Model whereas, the propaganda model (PM), as developed initially by Herman and Chomsky (1988), is a powerful reminder that the mainstream media are a crucial tool for legitimizing the ideas of the most powerful social actors and for securing consent for their actions.

Background of the Iraq War

The attack of the USA on Iraq was a preemptive attack to stop Iraq from manufacturing the WMDs. President Bush used the fake concept of 'Just War' for attacking a Muslim Arab hostile state. USA considered Iraq as an 'Axis of evil' along with Iran and N. Korea. The World wanted a clear justification of the USA attack in the Middle East. From the start, the principal challenge never was a matter of whether the U.S. military could topple Saddam Hussein's regime. Rather, the challenge has been all along with a matter of how to sell the war and U.S. military occupation to the community of nations, the United Nations Security Council, the American people, and the Iraqi people. So President Bush pushed the USA into 2nd war with Iraq and fulfilled his father's dream to topple Saddam Hussein. The post 9/11 was the scenario where he easily fulfilled his nefarious dream to bring change in Iraq.

The motive of the USA President was to show Iraq as a land of thugs, rapist and aggressor. According to the Ex-CIA Chief George tenant, President Bush was highly motivated to blame Iraq for the incident of 9/11 but he was unable to prove it. He got that chance in 2003 when on 6 March he delivered a speech which was totally against Iraq where he presented Iraq as an evil state. Bush constantly threatened Iraq and evoked the rhetoric of good and evil that he used to justify his crusade against bin Laden and Al Qaeda. Bush presented positioning himself against the "evil" that he was preparing to wage war against. Bush propagated that war against Iraq is for peace, the occupation of Iraq is its liberation, destroying its food and water supplies enables "humanitarian" action, and where the murder of countless Iraqis and destruction of the country will produce "freedom" and "democracy."

Propaganda as a tool in Iraq War

The most notorious country for the false flags operations is Israel but the US also has a long list of false flag operations organized by the USA Army and Intelligence agencies. On March 23, a story originated from an embedded reporter with the 'Jerusalem Post' that a "huge" chemical weapons production facility was found, a story allegedly confirmed by a Pentagon source to the Fox TV military correspondent who quickly spread it through the U.S. media. Grass lies were told to the world with the help of the Pentagon and CIA. Only USA causalities were shown. NBC CNN and Fox News were the main originators of the fake news. When the USA was presenting biased propaganda at that time the Canadian CBC and British BBC were presenting the near to reality details about the myth of WMDs. The USA broadcasting networks were presented a sanitized view of the war while Canadian, British and other European, and Arab broadcasting presented numerous images of civilian casualties and the horrors of war. U.S. television coverage showed their likeness toward pro-military patriotism, propaganda, and technological superiority.

The media propagated the links between al-Qaeda and Saddam Hussain. Unlike the sales campaign's companion issue of weapons of mass destruction, there was no logical or historical basis for believing that such an alliance existed. Saddam was a secular ruler and Al-Qaeda was a religious organization so there was no natural link between the two. To make people believe it a fictitious meeting in Prague was fabricated. The different propaganda techniques were devised to make people believe that Iraq is a part of the problem. The belief was cultivated by repeatedly uttering "Iraq," "9/11" and "war on terror" in the same breath. In the end, the majority of Americans believed that Saddam Hussein not only was allied with al-Qaeda but also had been directly involved in the 9/11 attack.

It is too early to judge the outcome from a very short distance and time. The narrative of the war is difficult to control. The media focused wrongly on casualties, looting and chaos, and U.S. military crimes against Iraqis rather than the U.S. victory and the evils of Saddam Hussein. The wrong narrative was built by propagandist against Iraq and its regime and the outcomes are very dangerous. The victory of the US in Iraq changes the destiny of that nation and plunged them into a sectarian war and perpetual unrest.

Conclusion

Propaganda is the most powerful tool in the arsenal of the hegemonic powers and they use it against their opponents. The USA used propaganda against the old-time enemy Iraq to start a war and the narrative was built to find excuses. 9/11 was missed but the story of WMDs was concocted and finally through propaganda the regime was malign and in the end overthrown. Now Iraq is more ethnically divided and sectarian than during the Sadam regime.

The War against Terror and Implementation of Geneva Conventions

Introduction

International Humanitarian Law (ILW) deals with the protection of humans during the crisis, especially in conflicts and wars. During the war, the soldiers are killed and the civilian population also comes under attack. During WWI and WWII millions of people were killed during these wars. To protect the prisoners of wars (POWs) from persecutions, prosecutions and atrocities, the Third Geneva Convention of POWs was passed and to date, it has been ratified by the 196 states.

Background

The Third Geneva Convention on POWs was first adopted after WWI in1929. The third Geneva Convention provides a wide range of protection for prisoners of war. It defines their rights and sets down detailed rules for their treatment and eventual release. International humanitarian law (IHL) also protects other persons deprived of liberty as a result of armed conflict. It was the result of the atrocities made during the armed conflict where enemy combatants were brutally tortured or murdered. According to estimates hundreds and thousands of POWs were killed due to starvation, torture and ill-treatment in the wars. After the end of WWI and WWII, millions of the German troops made as POWs and the majority of them were killed in camps when they were treated sub humanly. Millions of them were killed during the minesweeping operations which were forcefully performed by them during these wars.

The soldiers were always considered as the sons of the lesser gods, that's why millions of them became the prey of wars and after wars; they became the prey of the ill-treatment inflicted on them by the dominant successor force. After the end of WWII, the new treaty was signed by the states in 1949. Later on the Additional Protocol, I was signed in 1977.

POWs rights and War on Terror

International law is the name of a body of rules which regulate the conduct of the States in their relations with one another. Sources of international law include treaties, international customs, general principles of law as recognized by civilized nations, the decisions of national and lower courts, and scholarly writings. They are the materials and processes out of which the rules and principles regulating the international community are developed. The detention of the POWs is only done to prevent them from further participation in the conflict. The detaining power may prosecute them but under the International Humanitarian Law (IHL).

The USA started its war against terrorism after the 9/1 1incident, when they declared war against terrorism and they attacked Afghanistan in Oct 2001. The declared war ended with the fall of Kabul and the AL-Qaeda setup was dismantled. As a result of it, thousands of the Taliban and civilians were killed and a global hunt for fugitives was started. These prisoners were taken into USA custody and secretly shifted to Pakistan, Yemen, Syria, Egypt, Jordan and Eastern Europe for extraction of the information where they were badly tortured. The notorious prison of Guantanamo bay was erected. Article

2 specifies when the Convention is applicable. "First, it is applicable in all cases of declared war or of any other armed conflict which may arise between two or more of the High Contracting Parties even if the state of war is not recognized by one of them". This was violated by the USA and all the combatants were not declared as combatants and they were being deprived of all the basic rights.IHL also defines minimum conditions of detention covering such issues as accommodation, food, clothing, hygiene and medical care.

The fourth 1949 Geneva Convention and Additional Protocol I also provide extensive protection for civilian internees during international armed conflicts. If justified by imperative reasons of security, a party to the conflict may subject civilians to assigned residence or internment. Therefore, internment is a security measure, and cannot be used as a form of punishment. This means that each interned person must be released as soon as the reasons which necessitated his/her internment no longer exist. According to the different reports, different methods of torture were used against the 780 prisoners. Water-boarding, torture, rectal feeding, naked lynching, mock executions, sleep deprivation, stress positions, and other cruel and degrading treatment. Both in the Afghanistan and Iraq war USA deprived combatants of their laid down rights according to the Geneva Convention.

The prisoners were badly treated in Abu Ghraib and Bagram Base prison cells. A harrowing report from the US Senate revealed gruesome torture methods was applied against those prisoners. In non-international armed conflicts, Article 3 common to the 1949 Geneva Conventions and Additional Protocol II provide that persons deprived of liberty for reasons related to the conflict must also be treated humanely in all circumstances. In particular, they are protected against murder, torture, as well as cruel, humiliating or degrading treatment. Those detained for participation in hostilities are not immune from criminal prosecution under the applicable domestic law for having done so.

Conclusion

The USA is the sole superpower of the world. After the fall of the USSR, it was expected that now this world will become a land of peace because the eternal conflict between communism and capitalism was ended in1991. But post 9/11 incidents destroyed world peace and the fault lines between different religions and cultures were widening by the successive events. The sheer negligence was shown by the world's most powerful country while handling the non-state actors. The role of the UN was also not instrumental to safeguard the sovereignty of the countries against American aggression and its violations and transgression of the Geneva for the rights of the prisoners of war. The gruesome violations of human rights instigated many sympathizers to propagate against these atrocities and take up arms against the USA.

Middle East's Current Situation

Introduction

'Arab spring' started in Tunisia and ended in Egypt; its powerful shock waves destroyed all the status quo in the Muslim world and changed the dynamics of the world. It was a small disaster for the traditional Muslim world but its effects are very deep and powerful. The broad-based mobilization unleashed by these events continued after Mubarak's fall, underscoring the importance of the power of the street. Several theories in social science emphasize the role of de facto power, often resulting from groups being able to solve their collective action problems and mobilizing in the street, in changing economic allocations, and even in changing the de jure distribution of political power. Nevertheless, there is only limited evidence in economics and other social sciences showing that changes in the de facto political power of different groups and political mobilization directly matter for any economic outcome. The Arab Spring was a momentous set of changes, involving an unparalleled mobilization of people in many parts of the Arab world. In Egypt, it led to the downfall of the regime of Hosni

Mubarak, who had ruled the country as a de facto dictator for 30 years. In Yemen, Tunisia and Libya the regimes were toppled by the crazy street guys.

Present Muslim world

The current situation in the Middle East should persuade the people at the helm of affairs to rethink this false Endeavour. Many political thinkers have been speculating that the unrest would remain confined to the region. Whether the rest of the Muslim World would be spared from this kind of large scale popular revolt is an issue that calls for a separate examination, given its fragile social and political system and an almost stagnant economy. The relevant question now is that as the new Middle East evolves how this will affect the region's relations with the World.

Whatever pattern the current revolution will take, it is reasonable to argue that over time, the Middle East will never be the same again. In the meantime, they will try to defend the status quo in Bahrain, where their troops are now stationed to support the Sunni al-Khalifa family ruling over the Shia majority. If the Shias should win there, this would have repercussions concerning their Shia population, and will also boost Iran's position. Similarly, in Yemen, the president who has ruled the country for 32 years with an iron grip was getting support to resist change but brutally killed.

The current situation in the Middle East should persuade the people at the helm of affairs to rethink this false endeavour. Whatever pattern the current revolution will take, it is reasonable to argue that with time, the Middle East will never be the same again. To stem this tide the Saudi monarchy, for example, is beginning to sense the danger, but does not realize that offering stipends and subsidies will not meet the basic needs of the younger generation. Nor will the tokenism introduce municipal self-government. Then, there are questions about human rights, not only for the Shia minority but for women as well. The country needs social and economic reconstruction.

Egypt, not Saudi Arabia, holds a unique position in the Middle East and is destined to play an important role in the outcome in the region. How the revolution will play out in that country is difficult to answer. The movement can be in danger of getting compromised if elections are either too early or too late. And then the part the Muslim

Brotherhood would play would have a significant effect on the political structure which will replace the system developed by Hosni Mubarak. At present, the party is engaged in a vigorous internal debate about democracy and its place in the new political system in the country. It is important to note as well that with Mubarak removed from the scene, there will be no status quo ante for Israel.

Recent Developments

Looking at the rest of the Middle East, Algeria has an authoritarian regime and at present is living through a post-civil war trauma, which had bloody and cost around 200,000 casualties. Recently the government lifted the state of emergency. Morocco seems to have escaped this windstorm, with an accommodating monarchy and a stable political system. Jordan is trying to contain its unrest. The current main trouble spots are Libya and Syria. There are two notable regional players, Iran and Saudi Arabia, who have a direct stake in the changes which are taking place in the Middle East. And in the international arena, what role the US as well as China plan to pursue will have an important impact on the situation. All four of them have overlapping and conflicting objectives. The Middle East has always been an arena for this kind of diplomatic game.

Role of Foreign Powers

The US, for example, supports stability in Yemen and Bahrain from the point of view of its security. In Libya, however, it agreed to start the no-fly zone provided there was regional support for it. This was offered by the Arab League, where Saudi Arabia is an important member. In NATO, Turkey is a reluctant ally and supports an early ceasefire. If this should come to pass, then Libya would become a divided country, with rebels holding on to the areas on which they have gained effective control. How would China view this development will depend on how it can save its interest in Libyan oil, though it must be worried about the tottering of Middle East dominoes, representing authoritarian doctrines.

Hafez al-Assad established the regime with the liberalized but state-dominated economy, broadly on the Chinese model. The Ba'athist party has a strong grip on Syrian politics. Hafez al-Assad, for example, is known for having ruthlessly suppressed a revolt by Muslim Brotherhood when he bombed the city of Hama to kill about 35,000 people in 1982. Turkey's Tayyib Erdogan has advised Bashar al-Assad to implement the reforms without delay.

The Ba'athist party has a strong grip on Syrian politics. Hafez al-Assad, for example, is known for having ruthlessly suppressed a revolt by Muslim Brotherhood when he bombed the city of Hama to kill about 35,000 people in 1982. Bashar inherited the notorious emergency laws from his father's regime after his father's death in 2000. The civilian campaign is focused on these emergency laws. Turkey's Tayyib Erdogan has advised Bashar al-Assad to implement the reforms without delay. But like all the tyrants he is unwilling to implement the reforms. Saudia and Iran are playing tug of war in the Muslim world and the outcomes are very hilarious for the Muslims. In this situation, only a few Muslim countries are neutral like Pakistan, Malaysia and Turkey. These countries can play a game-changer role and can stop the Ripple effect of 'Arab spring' which has devastated the Muslim world. Western powers are playing the role of power brokers and disturbed the map of the Muslim world

Conclusion

There is complete confusion in Muslim World, Asia and Africa Stakes are high concerning the stability of Syria for Iran, a strategic ally of the country. It is through the Syrian medium that the Shia groups in Beirut get support from Iran, and Hamas is also a direct beneficiary of this arrangement. One could safely assume that Saudi Arabia is not going to escape the winds of change blowing across the entire Arab World. It would be in the interests of other Muslim States, to maintain the status quo in the region and partially support the emerging progressive forces in the Middle East.

Afghanistan Quagmire and USA Dialogue Efforts

Introduction

After the 9/11 incident USA decided to attack Afghanistan and started the most devastating long and costly war for itself. In October 2001 America started its attack on Afghanistan and dismantled the Taliban regime from Kabul with the help of the Northern Alliance. This long war has started showing very negative effects on the American economy in 2008 when the USA had shown the signs of slow down and the house mortgage bubble was blasted. After that President Obama announced his 'End Game' in Afghanistan but it was also partially failed because the American establishment was against it and they considered it too early. Now USA citizens are exhausted by this costly war and it is on the top Presidential campaign agenda.

Background of Taliban Movement

Taliban was a movement started by the young Madrassas students against the Soviet-era Mujahedeen. The Taliban emerged in 1994 as one of the prominent factions in the Afghan Civil War. From 1996 to 2001, the Taliban held power over roughly three-quarters of Afghanistan and enforced there a strict interpretation of Sharia or Islamic law. When the USA twin towers came under attacks, Al-Qaida and Taliban were blamed and the USA declared war against them in 2001 and the regime was changed. When the USA won that war and Kabul was occupied. Taliban started a guerilla war against the USA and its allies. In 2003 The North Atlantic Treaty Organization (NATO) assumes control of international security forces (ISAF) in Afghanistan, expanding NATO role across the country.

It is NATO's first operational commitment outside of Europe. NATO was originally tasked with securing Kabul and its surrounding areas, NATO expanded in September 2005, July 2006, and October 2006. The number of ISAF troops grew accordingly in the coming years. In 2018 after the first US troops entered Afghanistan, negotiations between the US and the Taliban began in earnest. The American delegation was led by the Afghan-born former US ambassador to Afghanistan, Zalmay Khalilzad. The Taliban delegation consists of a group of Taliban leaders led by Mullah Baradar, a co-founder of the group who was released from a Pakistani prison last year at the request of the US government.

Prospects of peace in Afghanistan

Since negotiations officially began last year, Taliban leaders have been released from prisons in Pakistan. International travel bans have been lifted to allow them to fly around the world for talks in Russia, Uzbekistan, and Qatar. In a country where as many as 35 million people are acutely focused on negotiations that will decide their fate, they're faced with an incredible lack of information about how the talks are proceeding. In 2018 USA and the Taliban started negotiation in Doha which concluded in the coming years. Trump administration opted to quit Afghanistan after all.

In 2019 negotiations between the United States and the Taliban in Doha enter their highest level yet, building on the momentum that began in late 2018. The talks between U.S. special envoy Zalmay Khalilzad and top Taliban official Mullah Abdul Ghani Baradar centred on the United States withdrawing its troops from Afghanistan in exchange for the Taliban pledging to block international terrorist groups from operating on Afghan soil. The ramped-up diplomacy follows signals that President Trump plans to pull out seven thousand troops, about half the total U.S. deployment. Khalilzad says the United States will insist that the Taliban agree to participate in an intra-Afghan dialogue on the country's political structure, as well as a cease-fire. It is unclear whether Trump will condition the troop withdrawal on those terms.

If America ceases to support the Afghan government, it's unlikely that other NATO partners will move to fill the void. The war in Afghanistan has cost America $3,714 per taxpayer since 2001, at a total cost of $737 billion which is a price tag that no government wants to take on for a war that many coalition partners have been quietly leaving for years. At its peak in the year 2012, the US government spent $97 billion in Afghanistan in one year. The dramatic increase in expenses after 2001 paid for more than just US military operations: It funded the invention and sustainment of one of the world's most corruption-riddled and vulnerable democracies: the Islamic Republic of Afghanistan. However, on September 7, 2019, President Trump announced that those talks, led by U.S. envoy Zalmay Khalilzad, had been called off. On November 28, 2019, President Trump made a surprise visit to Afghanistan, where he confirmed reports that unofficial talks had been restarted and claimed that the Taliban "want to do a ceasefire," prompting expressions of confusion by some Afghan government officials and denials from Taliban spokesmen.

Conclusion

Afghanistan was elevated as a significant U.S. foreign policy concern in 2001, the United States, in response to the terrorist attacks of September 11, 2001, led a military campaign against Al Qaeda and the Taliban government that harboured and supported it. In the intervening years, the United States has suffered around 2,400 military fatalities in Afghanistan and Congress has appropriated approximately $133 billion for reconstruction there." Until September 2019, U.S. military engagement in Afghanistan appeared closer to an end than perhaps ever before, as U.S. officials negotiated directly with the Taliban on the issues of counterterrorism and the presence of some 14,000 U.S. troops. Afghan government representatives have not been directly involved in U.S.-Taliban talks, leading some to worry that the United States would prioritize a military withdrawal over a complex political settlement that preserves some of the social, political, and humanitarian gains made since 2001. Observers speculate about what kind of political arrangement, if any, could satisfy both Kabul and the Taliban to the extent that the latter fully abandons armed struggle. Now it is in Biden's administration hands to deal with this complex situation and secure a way out from the Afghanistan quagmire.

Asia Pacific

ASEAN and BREXIT

Background

2016 was the decisive year where around 52 % of the British citizens opted to leave the EU. It was a massive blow for the Union and UK was the first country that officially opted to leave the organization. British Prime Minister David Cameron resigned from his office and PM Theresa May resumed the office. Although UK was not the founding member of the EU it was the leading economy of the group. This act of leaving the Union had deep-rooted impacts on the unity of the union. France and Germany had shown public resentment on this move but officially accepted the opinion of the British people. This phase of leaving the union was completed in the year 2020 when PM Boris Johnson signed the documents.

Britain and Splendid Isolation

Why British left this organization? is a million-dollar question. But first of all, we are the look into European history for the answer. Until the nineteenth century, the world order was revolved around the Balance of Power (BOP) concept where all the leading power of Europe tried to main the balance of power in the continent. In the 19th century, five European powers control the affairs of the world, British was one of them. Unluckily all these powers were Europe based. After the hundred years and thirty years of wars, European powers started the age of exploration and shifted their wars to the colonial grounds of Asia, Latin America and Africa. At that time British cut herself off from European affairs and went into splendid isolation. This age is also called "Pax Britannica".

What is regionalism?

According to the Oxford Dictionary "Regionalism" is a polysemic term that represents both a subfield of international relations (IR) that studies regions of the world and a process of formation of regions themselves". So "Regionalism" has many meanings. In IR we use this term to explain the integration of the regional states for some common causes i.e. trade or defence.

What is BREXIT?

In the referendum of June 2016, the British people with a razor-thin majority opted to leave the European Union. This was an unprecedented move for the EU. British PM David Cameron was in favour of the membership of the EU, so when the results came out he better left the office of the PM. After that, all the successive British governments negotiated with the EU for better Exit benefits and timeline.

The BREXIT and its Damage to Regionalism

In this contemporary world, there are few regional associations and organizations which are considered very successful i.e. ASEAN NATO NAFTA. Due to the BREXIT situation, there is a lot of confusions in the minds of the people about the future of these organizations.

UN and Regional Organizations

UN and its charter allow the regional organizations to operate in their areas. All the regional organizations are protected by the UN Charter but the use of force is strongly prohibited by the UN. ASEAN is a regional organization of South East Asia and considered the most successful organization of the Asian continent. All these are lawful organizations as per UN Charter

ASEAN and BREXIT

ASEAN is a successful trade organization of the region and after the BREXIT many people are showing doubts about the ASEAN. But ASEAN is completely a different organization, where all the states are free to operate and except trade, they deal with nothing. They are not dealing with the visa-free regime or soft border concepts. It is too early to conclude from the BREXIT that there is a shadowy future of regionalism.

Conclusion

So the BREXIT deal will not have any deep-rooted negative effects on the regional alliance and above all on the regionalism. Although there is uncertainty in the EU after this the success of Macron's pro-EU party in France has strengthened this stance that the future of regionalism is secure. The relations of EU are strategically secure and will flourish in the future. The EU's Foreign Policy chief, Federica Mogherini, has made clear to Asian partners that the EU seeks to be more embedded in the region. UK has not started a single dialogue after its membership of EU since 1973 but now it is a time when the UK will have to start new dialogues with WTO and ASEAN to secure its trade in the world.

Asian Colonialism in the Modern Era by MNCs

History of MNCs

The history of the multinational is linked with the history of colonialism. Many of the first multinationals were commissioned at the behest of European monarchs to conduct expeditions in Asia and Africa and Latin America. Many of the colonies not held by Spain or Portugal were under the administration of some of the world's earliest multinationals. One of the first arose in 1660: The East India Company, founded by the British. It was headquartered in London, and took part in international trade and exploration, with trading posts in India. Other examples include the Swedish Africa Company, founded in 1649, and the Hudson's Bay Company, which was incorporated in the 17th century. We are to keep in mind a few facts these MNCs were not established until the latter part of the nineteenth century. Large businesses invested abroad where and when their executives thought profits were to be made, not because of foreign policy concerns, and, with some exceptions, because they did not unduly seek to influence the formulation of foreign policy.

The influence of multinational corporations on foreign policy is complex, but, generally speaking, they have not played a major role in the formulation and execution of foreign policy. This may seem a surprising conclusion, but, indeed, MNCs are not directly involved in the formulation of foreign policies. They try to influence it for their financial benefits and tax evasions. WWI was the benchmark that forced the USA to come out of isolation and lead the world. The economic policies of President Woodrow Wilson (1913–1921) enunciated his concept of a 'new world order' predicated on classical liberal and capitalist principles. Due agricultural and industrial policies set the first phase of the expansion. These MNCs deployed different strategies to influence the target countries few are discussed here,

Financial/Technical Resources and Expertise There is no denying the fact that the MNCs bring in certain advantages to the host societies. Huge resources and investments, technology, innovation and expertise are made available to host societies through these MNCs. A culture of research and development, training in marketing and developing human resource within the organization utilized to influence the host countries through bribes etc.

Infrastructure Development Many MNCs help in improving the infrastructure and provision of basic needs in their specific areas of operation. They do it directly or provide funds to civil society organizations or give direct charity to improve the living and business conditions in areas where they are operating. These techniques make these MNCs that powerful that they can influence the people.

Credit Expansion The new credit culture is changing the attitudes towards loans. Loans are being encouraged to facilitate the acquisition of the luxuries of life. The offer of easy credit, consumer financing, credit cards and personal loans by the banks to the middle class is promoting a culture of living beyond means

Corruption and Crime Greediness, disparities and a sense of deprivation, along with the race to acquire new products are also giving rise to corruption and crime. On their part, MNCs also corrupt people and organizations to capture markets.

The hiring of Powerful People The term 'brain drain' is usually used for talent going towards other countries in search of higher income. MNCs have involved in yet another kind of brain drain. With their capacity to pay, they can hire the most qualified and experienced talent available in society. Those working with MNCs consider themselves as part of an elite class associated with the global community. Consequently, most of them develop a culture that makes them less relevant to their societies.

Trump's Foreign Policy and Asia

Background

When President Trump came into power in 2017, with election slogan was to make "America Great again". He is a descendent of a German family and his wife was born in Slovenia. From 2017 till 2020 he made all the possible somersaults in politics to make him relevant in politics. Trump is the main follower of "Social Darwinism" and his major policies revolve around his concept of ethnic and racial segregation of different people. In the coming paragraph, we will discuss in detail that how Trump has destroyed the international image of America. Although he is the first President in the recent past that has not started a single war, still his image has been tarnished internationally. First of all, we will discuss the list of achievements of President Trump which are as under.

Achievements of Trump Administration

Here are few achievements of President Trump:

(a) Taliban Deal After a long and hectic dialogue with the Taliban in February 2020. The USA signed a Peace Agreement with the Taliban. The Afghan government was taken into confidence and the USA accepted the demand of the Taliban to systematically withdraw the troops from Afghanistan. It can be considered the biggest success of President Trump.

(b) A New Mideast Deal Under the pressure of the Trump administration Bahrain and UAE normalized relations with Israel. The USA was expecting that around five Muslim countries will accept Israel including Sudan, Oman and Tunis. It was an unprecedented success of the Trump administration. Palestinian Authority was very sceptical about this USA move.

(c) Thaw with North Korea Trump attempted to attack North Korean leader by calling him the "Missile Man" and making him the media mockery. Later on, Trump became the 1st USA President to visit North Korea. Although this visit brought nothing special for the US it was the 1st step towards nothing special for the US but it was the 1st step towards ice-breaking between the two belligerent states.

(d) Syrian Fiasco Although Trump was not the first who started this war nor he was the last one who ended it, but his failure in the resolution of the Syrian affair gave time to Russia to break the backbone of the western supported ISIS in Syria. This resulted in avoiding another humanitarian crisis.

(e) Rapprochement with Russia Trump became the fierce admirer of Russian President Putin. FBI and USA media had continuously blamed the role of Russian intelligence in the 2017 elections. Trump had a different approach towards Russia. During his tenure, Russia occupied the South of Ukraine through its proxies. No new confrontation was started with Russia and deal relations with Russia were there.

(f) Mitigated war expenditures Trump lowered the war expenditures in Iraq and Afghanistan. At the peak time of the war, the US was consuming the US $ 1 Trillion per annum on these wars. He started the negotiation process and signed a peace agreement with the Taliban. He demanded money from Japan and South Korea for keeping troops in the Pacific region.

Failures of Trump Administration

With few achievements, many failures were made by the Trump administration, which are

(a) Withdrawal from TPP When the Obama administration presented the "Asia Pivot Policy" at that time the USA focused Pacific region as the No one priority area. USA signed twelve members Trans-Pacific Partnership (TPP) but Trump withdrew from the deal in 2017. It was a complete setback for the policymakers in Washington.

(b) Travel Ban on Muslims Trump imposed a ban on the travellers coming from the six Muslim countries to enter the USA. It was a complete blow for a Superpower and its prestige. Humanitarian organizations put pressure on Trump but all in vain.

(c) Left Paris Accord For the protection of the climate and environment USA signed Paris Accord to have cut on carbon emissions but unilaterally the USA withdrew from the agreements which created an International uproar against its superpower role. The USA sidelined itself from international obligations.

(d) Not ratified Iran Deal Obama brokered a nuclear deal with the help of European powers with Iran. West was considering it as its feast but Trump rubbished the nuclear deal and left Iran lurking. Iran started enriching the Uranium in its plants. IAEA, Russia and France were astonished by this decision.

(e) Chinese trade war Trump started a trade war with China and imposed a ban on products by tariffs and non-tariff barriers. Billions of dollars duties were imposed on China. These duties have reciprocated China, which was changed into a trade war.

(f) Great Wall of America Trump made an election promise to construct a wall along its eastern border with Mexico. After coming into power Trump demanded the US $ 5.7 billion for the wall construction.

(g) Dealing with Corona Virus The biggest failure for the Trump administration was its dealing with the Corona Pandemic. CDC and Dr Fuci played a significant role but it was overshadowed by the childish acts of Trump. On the other hand, China emerged as the better administrator to deal with the virus.

Conclusion

The list of Trump's failure is longer than its achievements. He was a president who had more than 32 million Twitter followers and he was notorious to made official announcements through Twitter. He would be remembered in history that he instigated his followers to attack a capitol building where five people were killed. The tenure of Trump was full of uncertainty and it decreased the American international influence. It also has shown the shallowness of the new international order where the USA was playing the role of a superpower. The trade war with China was started by Trump and he baldy dealt with the Corona Virus which created international hue and cry.